# My Life in Seven Languages

*A Linguistic Memoir*

George P. Fletcher

Mazo Publishers

# My Life in Seven Languages

ISBN: 978-1-936778-97-3



*Contact the Author*
Email: GeoPFletcher@aol.com

*Published by:*
Mazo Publishers
*Website*: www.mazopublishers.com
*Email*: cm@mazopublishers.com
Tel: 1-815-301-3559

*For all those who have listened patiently and spoken slowly*

*A special thanks to Herbert Morris and Robert Cooper*
*for encouraging me in this project*
*and working with me on the manuscript.*

# Contents


Introduction 6

*Chapter One*
Youthful Stimuli 10

*Chapter Two*
Learning German 20

*Chapter Three*
My First Mission: Russian 53

*Chapter Four*
My Family: Hungarian 78

*Chapter Five*
Love: Spanish 114

*Chapter Six*
My People: Hebrew 134

*Chapter Seven*
My Son: French 152

*Chapter Eight*
My Calling: English 163

# Introduction

At an early age, my father, Miklós, taught me an expression very popular among Hungarians: *Ahány nyelv, annyi ember*. Liberally translated: You are as many people as languages you speak. If someone speaks to you in a language you don't understand, and you have a plausible chance to learn that language and you don't, you are a lesser person. This always made sense to me, maybe because my father taught it to me. It was quintessentially Hungarian. The theory is that a small people in Central Europe, saddled with a language so difficult to learn, so hard to understand, will inevitably learn the major languages of literature and commerce. One is reminded of the Pest from Budapest in *My Fair Lady*. He was good at languages and, even more importantly, at bluffing.

The truth is that the competence of Hungarians at foreign languages is overrated. When I looked around the immigrant generation of my aunts and uncles, I saw Hungarians who spoke, in addition to their native language, fairly weak English. In my generation, born in the US, only two of us – my cousin Paul and I – bothered to take foreign languages seriously.

Looking back at my use of time in the course of my 70 years, I am struck by the extraordinary amount of time I devoted to making lists of new words in foreign languages, learning them by heart, and practicing them whenever I could. I also have cherished friendships with men and women who have expressed themselves in languages other than English. It is not easy to stick to another tongue when your friend speaks the now dominant language of the world. That is why most people who speak fluent English draw their friends into their linguistic orbit.

Benjamin Lee Whorf wrote a series of books in which he argued that our language influences the way we think. This is one of those claims that makes you think there is something to it but it is nonetheless impossible to verify. He concentrated on verbs of action in American Indian languages, the claim being that the concept of action was different. The hypothesis is difficult to validate or refute. When investigators work with subjects who speak other languages, we don't know how or what they would think if they spoke the investigator's language. In any event, you can imagine the kind of arguments generally welcomed under this proposition. They are more subtle than the conventional points about the Eskimos' having more words for white or for snow than we have. I assume this point about vocabulary is true because different linguistic cultures have a different set of experiences, which probably adds nuance to the perceptions of daily life.

The influence of language on thought is one of those propositions whose validity is somewhere between zero and 100%, but you don't know where on the scale it falls. We have a similar problem in the law. We know that the law influences the decisions of judges but we cannot determine how much. It is somewhere between zero and total effect. It might be that in the area of mind and thought we can never get it right. If not, there is some value to looking at the problem from the inside, from the standpoint of individuals trying to use their minds in particular ways.

The use of the mind that interests me here is speaking – formulating words and sentences. If there is anything that is distinctively human – something beyond the capacity of other animals and computers – it is creating the infinity of forms in living languages. Perhaps you could compute the number of words and sentences used in Latin when it was spoken and come out with a finite number, but you could never do that in a language that potentially expands every time it is used. It is not easy to grasp that the languages we speak are infinite in form – for how could we grasp them and think we dominate them if they were infinite and constantly expanding? Some people may use few words but they are always capable of understanding a new word when an imaginative advertiser or humorist throws one at them.

In this book I will write about language from the inside – from my perspective growing up in seven infinities. It is not easy to imagine dominance over seven undefined, constantly expanding fields of words and sentences; therefore the only way to make it plausible is to tell the story from the standpoint of experience. I am interested in the impact of these languages on my relationships with other people. Does French make me more inclined to amorous feelings? Does Hebrew make me feel greater solidarity with others? Does Hungarian make me see the world as would the Rubik cubist, as a set of interlocking spatial relations? Is there anything to the Russian talk about their *dusha*, their mysterious emotional soul different from others?

In an era when foreign languages are studied and matter less in building a career, it might simply be interesting to understand what it has been like for an American born during World War II to live a life in seven languages. By living a life, I mean just that – as indicated by establishing serious relationships in the language, teaching a class in the language, trying a legal case in the language, or having some other intensive experience that goes beyond the level of tourism and ordering in restaurants. I have an additional number of languages that fit into the tourist category – Japanese and Italian – but they are beyond the scope of this book. Discussing seven should be enough.

There are many different ways to reflect over the rich 70 years I have devoted to playing, working, and loving. Each of these activities could provide a focal point for organizing a memoir. In our culture, there is the tendency to organize life into segments based on marriages, relationships, jobs, or perhaps other momentous life-changing challenges – wars, illnesses, suffering. It turns out that in each of my languages, I have had close personal relationships, often fallen in love, and been active as a lawyer in foreign courts. However enriching these experiences were to me, they strike me as a spin-off from my love of the language. *My Life in Seven Languages* consists of a series of cross-sectional probes into events – marriages, legal cases, friendship, intellectual pursuits – that would normally be told as single events dominating all aspects of the time in which they occur. But the fact is that for me, the linkage between trying a case in Russian and falling in love in Russian provides the relevant way of organizing experiences. The linguistic dimension dominates and organizes these events in a way that would never occur to someone for whom the element of language lies in the background.

My legal experience in seven different cultures typically had political overtones. That makes sense. For the most part, these are not cases in which my client just chose me from a list of available advocates. They came to me through lawyers, typically lawyers abroad who realized that their client had a politically sensitive case and that some special talent was necessary to defend him properly. Because of my particular expertise in foreign legal systems, they reached out to me.

In order to become the lawyer who could serve in these foreign cases, I had to learn languages. I am grateful to all the native speakers who had to tolerate me in the early days of my learning a new language. Typically, I imitated Eliezer ben Yehudah, the man credited with reviving modern Hebrew, by switching to a language and pretending to know no other. This is annoying sometimes to the people who would rather speak English. Sorry, there is no other way to learn a new language.

Chapter One

# Youthful Stimuli

My early childhood was a cacophony of different language registers. My parents and my family spoke Hungarian, virtually all the time. My sister Lillian, nine years older than I, spoke only Hungarian before she encountered the kids on the street and came home bawling because they were of a different world.

My playmates on the street a few years later all spoke Greek at home. The Near North Side of Chicago was their territory. Their families were ahead of ours because they encouraged their children to speak English outside of the home yet insisted on Greek at home. It helped that their church conducted prayers in Greek, too. I never had an inkling, until later, that their familial language was different from mine.

The day that a neighbor opened his window and shouted down to us, "Hey kids, you know Roosevelt is dead," we all understood. Curiously, I could barely read, but I understood the political significance of this event. My best explanation is that my father listened to Edward R. Murrow's radio broadcast every night. I knew about the war, but only the better part of it – when we were winning. I was too young to understand the depressive mood of the family before Stalingrad. The news improved with my vocabulary. My childhood was a curve of ascending

*The Fletcher family – ca. 1945.*

expectations.

My first sense that there was a fascinating world beyond my linguistic ken crystalized when my parents took a trip at the end of the war to visit my father's siblings in the southern cone of Latin America. We received calls from Buenos Aires and Havana. The crackling tone of my parents' voices on the other end of the line excited my six-year-old imagination. Then I saw the pictures of my parents with friends and relatives in these exotic places. They were all wearing formal outfits and walking in the city plaza or against the backdrop of imposing old buildings. They gave me a sense that these faraway places represented a higher level of style and civilization than my humble barrio. My mind was beginning to awaken to the great world of travel beyond the boundaries of

*Fanny and Miklós in Buenos Aires.*

Winnemack Avenue and River Park.

The boundaries would not burst, however, until my father Miklós landed in the hospital with a heart condition. He had worked too hard in his youth, my mother Fanny said. He worked on the docks in Europe. He worked on construction in Chicago. He painted houses to support his family. At the outset he did not have a clue about how to do any of these things. He would show up in the morning and imitate the other guys until he got fired. What could any of us expect? Miklós was born on a large estate on the outskirts of Szécsény, Hungary, and grew up riding horses and flirting with gypsies. When his coronary arteries narrowed, the doctor had a remedy, the same that he offered to dozens of patients at the time: Broaden your life. Go West, where the sun is bright and the lawns stay green all year. My mother was convinced and made the decision for us. She had enough money to go out to Los Angeles, confer with the local Hungarian Jews about what a good business might be, and when she got the unscientific tip "Hotels look good," she could put a down payment on the Regina Hotel near Alvarado and Sixth Street, next to the now junkie-ridden green called MacArthur Park.

The great migration brought us into a part of the country where Spanish and English had not resolved their respective claims to dominance in the popular culture. The journey to Los Angeles, which lasted more than a week, had me gawking out the car window at sights I had never seen before. There were no superhighways then, and virtually no motels, certainly no chains of restaurants or hotels with reliable conditions. The roadside was mostly farms and countryside, lots of local eateries, not a fast food joint in sight. It was a different, more colorful America.

The comfort level was minimal. One night we had to flee a hotel in the dark because one of our party started screaming about fleas in the bed sheets. This was high adventure for a seven-year-old.

Because of his illness, my father went ahead by train. We drove into Salt Lake City and there we came upon him while he was out for his daily constitutional. We caught sight of him as he was crossing the street. Serendipities in the Great American West! He finished the trip by car with us. We rolled into LA together and found our way to the parking lot of the Regina Hotel.

The first summer in LA – my last summer of linguistic innocence – we spent in the modest luxury of the Regina Hotel, with its garden and swimming pool. I went to the park every day, fed the birds, and rode around in the rowboats. I see now that I enjoyed a high level of freedom for a seven-year-old. My parents put me in art school because – God knows why – they thought I had talent, but I did not last long. I was beginning to develop a will to counteract the plans made by others.

My father's partner in the hotel – a man named Kovács – had bought a magnificent, four-story house on the top of a hill in Glendale. Every child's dream, it was equipped with secret compartments and hidden crannies to hide your money and perhaps your friends and travelers in trouble. Had it been in a different location, it could be best described as suited to be part of the underground railway in the Civil War. We rented it for a year and

*George, ready to begin his journey.*

moved in September, just in time for me to register in the Glenoaks public school down in the flats of Glendale.

The first week in school tested my newly-emergent will to run my own life. Because of my birthday in early March, the Chicago school system decided I should start kindergarten in the middle of the year. By the time I left Budlong School in Chicago, I had completed the first half of the second grade, namely 2A but not 2B. But like all California schools, the Glendale schools began every class in the fall. The second half of the second grade was offered only in the spring. For me, therefore, the assignment was to be either second grade or third grade. The Glendale administrator naturally wanted to put me back in 2A, and I think most kids would have accepted it – less work, more leadership possibilities, a chance to be dominant. In my case there was an additional reason – I was small for my age. But my emergent will made up for my modest appearance. If I had heard of a hunger strike at that age, I would not have ruled it out in my persistence to go with the older boys and girls. I was not going to allow myself to "fail" a half year – at least it seemed that way. They decided to let me try 3A – the first great payoff of deciding things for myself.

There was only one big hurdle, which apparently did not enter into the principal's considerations. Someplace between 2A and 3A, the Glendale kids learned cursive handwriting. I did not have a clue how to do this. I could print and read and do my sums, but I could not write in the elegant connected style – which apparently has atrophied in American education. My wonderful teacher – God bless her for this and the item I shall mention next – let me stay after school to practice handwriting. I caught up with the class within a couple of weeks.

Her great virtue was not her tolerance for my obdurate will, but her courageous decision to introduce the entire class to Spanish. I do not believe this was part of the curriculum because for the rest of my years in California public schools – until the ninth grade – no teacher ever came close to teaching us a foreign language. She taught us how to count, the names of holidays, some basic expressions. The project was not only Spanish but the study of the entire Spanish culture in California. We celebrated the Mexican holidays – I remember dancing with sticks around the piñata on the fifth of May – and we made long bus trips to the Spanish missions in Southern California. The great meaning of this, I believe, was that we were celebrating the "other" in California. I had no reason to think that Spanish culture was superior to our own. We were taught to respect another great culture and the history of the place we were in. This stands in contrast to the general attitude of the schools in those days. I remember being offended a few years later when I encountered a picture of a "typical" Mexican in a textbook – sleeping under a tree with his sombrero shielding his eyes. Today, I imagine, political correctness has taken over, and there are no pictures of that sort, but I doubt that respect for the Spanish language could be taught with the same zeal as in that offbeat third grade class in the flats of Glendale.

When we still lived in the Glendale house, my father's mother arrived one day. She had survived the mass killings by the Nazis in 1944, ensconced, as my mother said, in a famous villa in Budapest. Now she was on her way to live with her family in Santiago, Chile (more about them later). She encountered me one day in the garden but I could not communicate with her. The problem was not so much the lack of news or other topics of conversation. But the point for me, then as it is now, was language. She only spoke Hungarian and I did not. I suffered a deep sense of shame in not having learned Hungarian, the family language, as a child – when learning a language occurs without even noticing it. I am sure that this shame is the source of a not entirely rational attitude that I developed later in life: When I meet a new person, I should not assume that they speak my language. And if they speak a different language, I must learn at least a few words of it.

After my exposure to Spanish vocabulary in class, the Mexican games, and the bus trips to great centers of Catholic missionary work, I understood that I would have to speak Spanish to those who spoke Spanish. They and my grandmother were my first contact with those with whom I did not share a language. They were the "others." The deeper point that seeped in, however, was that I was also one of the others. I would be the one at the center of communication. I realized for the first time that my parents did not speak English to each other. They were not speaking Spanish at home either. They had to make a leap across a linguistic divide to speak to their son. When they lapsed back into Hungarian, I started paying attention to their expressions and imitating my father's favorite curse words.

For a seven-year-old, far from turning eight, this was an explosion of universes. It energized my imagination. But there was also a dark side to it all. Neither Spanish nor Hungarian was the language of insults that triggered fighting in the school yard and in the streets. That year I learned to fight. The kids on the bus and in the schoolyard started taunting me about being Jewish. I did not have a clue what "Jewish" meant but they did, or rather their parents told them that Jews were not welcome in the neighborhood. That was all very complicated to me because I could not fit the label "Jewish" into the categories of language that I was learning to use to interpret the world.

I had no clue whether the other kids were Catholic or Protestant and it did not matter. They had no idea why they should take their parents seriously about hating Jews. The entire game was reduced to a ritual. They called me a name like "dirty Jew" and I had to fight. If I did not fight, I was a coward, which was much worse than anything that could be attributed to Jews. The amazing thing is that with little experience, I learned how to defend myself. Of course, in those days, fighting meant wrestling. No rocks, no knives. This was not West Side Story. It was not an ethnic struggle, but the tale of one newcomer trying to be part of the group. Winning consisted in getting the other guy to say "uncle." This would usually happen as a result of a hammer lock or a body press. Fists were used sparingly. No one really wanted to hurt anyone else. When I won, we were all friends. When one of them won, there was always another fight on the horizon. I wished the Middle East today worked on the same easy principle of pre-teenage boys.

My career in Spanish did not go far at the Glenoaks School. But something important happened: I understood that there was a culture out there beyond me; in my father's idiom, there was a person I was not.

In the following summer of 1947, when I was eight years old, my parents moved into a house at 205 South Swall Drive in Beverly Hills. It had a large tree in the backyard, and all I could think about was building a tree house in the tree and hanging out there reading comic books. My parents thought it better to enroll me in a Jewish summer camp right around the corner on Wilshire Boulevard. I did not object. I wanted the chance to meet some new kids. Of everything we did and learned, nothing much stuck except one ditty in Hebrew that went like this.

*Zoom, Golly, Golly, Zoom, Golly, Golly,*
*CheChalutz l-man Ha-avodah, Ha-avodah l-man CheChalutz.*

The first line is a nonsense ditty to set the rhythm. The second line is very serious. It means: "The Pioneer (Chalutz) is made for work (Avodah) and work (Avodah) is made for the Pioneer (Chalutz)."

As an Israeli friend, Yoram Shachar, noted to me recently,

they were teaching us not only Zionism, but socialist Zionism. Surprisingly, many of my native-born Israeli friends are not familiar with the little song that was my first connection with these new concepts of work and nationalism.

Largely because I insisted on understanding it, the song fueled my imagination both about languages and the adventure of settling a new land. There was another moral world – a world where pioneers lived by a different ethic. Some of these Zionist ideals were confirmed by the work my mother was putting together in an organization called Shelters for Israel, a charitable group for Hungarian Jews that had the purpose of building new housing in Israel. They built the first housing units in Kiryat Ono, a suburb of Tel Aviv. Perhaps the real reason for the organization was to hold nice parties called "fund-raising" events. No matter, I enjoyed the parties and the Zionist message eventually took hold in me.

For the next four years in the Beverly Hills schools, I did not learn much of value. My yearning for Spanish identity and a kindling of interest in Hebrew went into remission. My conscious mind was occupied by learning the petty skills of spelling, math, geography, and one thing I did love – American history. The conflict with the Spanish-speaking world was, of course, always at the top of the agenda. For me, the struggle was not with Indians but with the Spanish. I read American history as a great battle of competing languages for the heartland of the United States. German had an edge for a while in Pennsylvania. Spanish rode hard in the Southwest, but gradually, with little wit and even less wile, the English language became the language of instruction in the schools across the country.

There are basically two ways that young people learn to speak more than two or three languages. Sometimes they are forced by the circumstances of their youth to move from one language system to another and to learn to speak a new language, as I learned cursive writing, in order to keep up with their class. I know many immigrant children who have been through this experience. A good example is my friend Michel Rosenfeld, a law professor in New York. Growing up in Mexico City, he went to a French school and spoke Hungarian at home. English came as a matter of course. He never had to make a deliberate choice to learn these languages. I think this is typical of those who learn by the fortuities of where they live and who their parents are. Those exposed to the necessity of a multilingual life rarely develop the kind of love for foreign languages that will lead them to tackle new and difficult languages – like Russian or Japanese. They are fortunate to hold on to the few languages they know. It is a gift they take for granted rather than an invitation to continue voluntarily to study that which they were forced to learn by the pressure of circumstances.

I put myself into another category of language learners – those who learn by passion rather than by the contingencies of travel and residence. My education was in English from the age of 5 to 24. I was never forced to learn another language, and yet somewhere in these early experiences in Chicago and Glendale – Hungarian at home, Greek in the neighborhood, Spanish in school, and my first Hebrew words in a Zionist song, I discovered a world that beckoned a commitment on my part. I was not going to learn by involuntary exposure. I had to make a conscious choice to master the words and phrases that would enable me to realize my father's ideal: *Ahány nyelv annyi ember* – The more languages you know, the more personalities you have.

It was not easy to develop the will and the discipline to learn languages, but without it I would be limited to a smattering of words in the language as are many who take courses in high school and college but never force themselves to function in the language. Going beyond school and family requires great determination. How I developed that will and how it influenced my professional ambitions, my friendship, my love life – this is the story I have to tell.

Chapter Two

# Learning German

I did not know much about the German language and I did not know anything about how to learn a language before I was thirteen, when I started the ninth grade at Beverly Hills High School.

As any self-conscious Eastern European Jews would have done, my parents told me that among my choices (German, French, Spanish, Latin) there was no doubt that I should sign up for German. Their respect for the language was uncanny. They did not speak more than a few words of it. They didn't know the closely related Yiddish language, yet their way of defining themselves as Hungarian Jews, despite the Holocaust, was to remain loyal to German culture.

I entered Mr. Knauer's class with a great sense of enthusiasm. (Interestingly, he is one of the two teachers from my high school years whose name I remember.) From the first day, I found the material easy to master and took with great alacrity to the entire process. German grammar is much like American grammar, only more complicated. It has three genders of the nouns (*der, die* and *das* – masculine, feminine and neuter) and each of these genders declines in four different cases, each case dependent on its role in the sentence – nominative as subject, genitive as a possessive, dative as indirect object, and accusative as direct object. And then there are rules about prepositions – some take one case of the noun, others take another case, and still others shift back and forth, depending on whether the sentence describes location or destination. I found all of this fascinating. The challenge was not only the logic of the grammar but the mastery I could display by memorizing the tables and the charts governing the whole system. My learning to master German became the template for my subsequent mastery of other languages.

It is hard for me to know how much I learned from Mr. Knauer and how much from later study of the language. He had a deep love of the language, which he managed to communicate to us despite the bias against Germany seven years after the war. He implicitly made it clear that language was not political and we proceeded from there. The curriculum followed popular German culture. We read well-known books for children like *Emil und die Detektive* by Erich Kaestner. I am not sure how far we would have had gotten if my education in German had not been cut short by my family's moving from Beverly Hills to Hollywood. I made the major mistake of transferring to the much inferior Hollywood High, which had a very bad German teacher and only offered two years of the subject. After the summer of 1954, I was essentially on my own in learning German. Somehow I kept it up. On a trip through Europe in 1962, I found that I could communicate about basic matters fairly well *auf Deutsch* – at least in Germany, Switzerland and Eastern Europe.

## *The Long Break and the Big Break*

Nothing happened to take my interest in Germany beyond the tourist level until 1963, when I was finishing law school and had no clue about what I would do. I knew that I did not want to go to work in a law firm. I didn't think I could handle the office life and the obligatory submission to people of authority. I would have enjoyed prosecuting criminal cases, although I did not know it at the time. I basically liked studying but I was not first in my law school class of 150 – or even close – so I could not get a clerkship to the Supreme Court, which was the preferred way of doing what

I wanted to do – namely, enter academic life. My professors barely noticed me among the other bright and eager students. Yet I had some good luck. Despite my dubious grades, I was able to write my way onto the law review, that is, I wrote an essay that made up for the deficiencies in my grades. The older students took a liking to me. I remember all the late night sessions in the library with John Junker, Gerald Witherspoon and Steve Talent. Junker taught me how to write by forcing me to rewrite my comment for the law review ten times. I am forever grateful.

Then I met a charming professor named Max Rheinstein who paid attention to students who knew a few languages. Rheinstein was one of the German-Jewish immigrants who enormously enriched American law schools in the period from 1950 to 1975. They were the first generation who, as a group, preached the necessity of studying comparative law. In their sophisticated perspective, it was hardly sufficient to learn the law in English and in English-speaking countries. It was necessary to branch out and to explore the critical differences and similarities among legal systems in a variety of languages. Max, as we affectionately called him, was a very learned man, though with a rather conventional mind. He differed from fellow immigrant Albert Ehrenzweig out at Berkeley, who had a revolutionary mind and set out to transform the foundations of American law. The difference between them was that Ehrenzweig was from Vienna and brought with him the most radical ideas of Freud and the *fin de siecle*. Rheinstein was from Munich, a comfortable *buergerliche Stadt,* known for *Oktoberfest* and beer hall speeches, but not much more. (Well, there was that little man with a mustache and an odd part in his hair). Rheinstein defended and taught Munich law. This included the grandeur of the BGB, the civil code, and the conventional ideas of 1962 about building the European Union.

Rheinstein had a precursor at the University of Chicago, who furthered the consciousness of the school about the importance of learning German law. His name was Karl Llewellyn, one of the greatest figures of American law in the 20th century. He was born in Seattle of Welsh heritage, taught himself German and went to Germany to study. It was of enormous interest to us students that he fought on the German side in the First World War (as my father had done in the Austrian-Hungarian Army) and then came back to academic work in the United States. One of his early books, in German, explained the American system of precedent to a German audience. But his methods were not essentially tied to the German language or German law. He wrote another book called *The Cheyenne Way* (with the anthropologist E.A. Hoebel) which was about law in that distinguished tribe. With the spirit of Karl Llewellyn in the institution, almost any innovative program was possible. The Ford Foundation, under the guidance of Max Rheinstein, decided wisely to invest its funds in the Chicago Law School's vision of comparative law. They established a two-year program – the first year in an intensive seminar with Max on either French or German law and the second year abroad, in a program of the student's choice. Mary Ann Glendon, now a distinguished scholar and professor at Harvard, took the program the year before me when the emphasis was on French law. I was fortunate that the wheel turned to German law in my year, first because my German was better than my French and second, because German law was Rheinstein's true love and, in my impression, the more sophisticated legal system (sophisticated legal systems can, of course, engage in enormous evil).

There were six of us in the program. We met every morning for an 8 a.m. seminar. The others were rather clever, I thought, but no one seemed to be headed for an academic career. The closest was Walker Miller, who went on to Freiburg with me. He ended up as a judge in Colorado, with, so far as I know, a very satisfying career. I had an unusual affection for the theoretical side of the civil code, the BGB, and I quickly discovered my innate loyalty to academic argument. Rheinstein brought over a young assistant from Germany named Ulrich Drobnig, who later became head of the Max Planck Institute in Hamburg. Drobnig was very German and could not stand American habits – everything from our way of sitting in class to our manners when we went out to drink a beer. He told us frankly what he thought, which turned out to be excellent preparation for confronting the rigid systems of social interaction still dominant in German culture. I quickly learned that Germans had rules about when and with whom you had to shake hands, about forms of address, about levels of intimacy (*Sie und Du*), about the proper size and shape of red and white wine glasses, etc.

The more I learned about these manners, the more I adopted them and enjoyed them. They reminded me very much of my parents' fealty to some of the same gestures – particularly those between men and women. As far as my mother was concerned, a man's extending his hand first to a woman was a sin. Even worse was walking up a set of stairs behind a woman (he might look up her dress). Equally bad for the Germans was drinking white wine out of a red wine glass or vice versa. My sense is that Americans are oblivious to these rules. The first time I noticed an American man extending his hand to a woman, I was truly shocked.

One incidental benefit of the graduate year in Chicago was that I had occasion to take a few courses in economics, which brought me into contact with one of my great heroes in the field, Friedrich von Hayek, who was known as the leader of the Austrian liberal theory of economics. He also wrote a few interesting books about jurisprudence. In one, he compared the legal system to the market: case law supposedly sought equilibrium in the way prices do. This is far-fetched but interesting. Hayek provided an important link between my year in Chicago and the subsequent year in Freiburg. I went to his class there and then he invited me to lunch, just the two of us, at the Columbi Hotel in the center of town. I felt so honored I dedicated myself to reading everything that he has ever written – at least of relevance to jurisprudence.

I chose Freiburg because I thought it was stronger at criminal law than in other subjects. Freiburg was the location of the Max Planck Institute in International and Foreign Criminal Law. I had a deep romantic attachment both to the mysteries of crime and punishment. The criminal was a kind of hero for me – the spirit who broke loose from the conventional bounds of his milieu – though, as I learned later, often motivated by the respect of his peer group. Punishment too had a brutal romance to it: it created a situation that tested the capacity of human beings to resist their humiliation and the deprivation of their liberty. For many years, films about prison life and prison breaks held me in great fascination.

I did not know much about Freiburg except the name of the institute of criminal law. I had no idea that Freiburg would turn out to be so charming, comfortable, and engaging that I would develop a life-long attachment to the city.

Yet the year in Freiburg did not turn out to be as easy as I expected. First, my textbook German collided against the local dialect spoken in Baden. The locals had trouble understanding me, not the least reason for which was that I spoke in the academic idiom of the BGB. My language sounded like that of an Englishman, fresh from a mediaeval law library, who enters a bar and says, "I pray, may it beseech thee to offer me a contained but uncapped body of alcoholic fluids." Perhaps this is an exaggeration but there were some pretty funny incidents in my first few weeks of speaking German on the spot.

The more difficult part of the year was that for the first time I had to confront my Jewish identity. I had probably not thought about being Jewish since my first year in Beverly Hills when I learned my first few words of Hebrew. My cousin Paul, who is close to me in age and lifestyle, had a good Jewish education and even thought about becoming a rabbi. This was a major divergence between us in our early years.

Less than a generation after the war's end, the residue of National Socialism was everyplace in Freiburg. Though the city had been rebuilt (it had not suffered much bombing in the first place) there were other reminders of nostalgia for Hitler's politics. The city was dotted with signs that read: *Drei geteilt: niemals* (Divided in three parts, never!). It took me a long time to figure out what that meant. The three parts, apparently, were the Federal Republic of Germany, the Democratic Republic of Germany, and the territory now in Poland, east of the Oder/Neisse line. All of this land had been part of Hitler's Reich. In other words, the war had not changed anything. The German Reich was entitled to the same territory that it had when Hitler took power. Eventually, of course, both Germanys had to surrender the lands east of the Oder/Neisse lines to Poland and were forced to live in de facto mutual recognition until 1990.

But this was hardly the worst part of my living as a Jew in a territory that had been ruled by Nazis only 20 years before I arrived. There were still many people around with unreconstructed anti-Semitic attitudes. My wife Susan was pregnant and we did not know whether the child who would be born in September would be a boy or a girl. We inquired about a *briss,* a ritual circumcision, for the possible boy. No one had a clue how this might be done, but the mere mention of the word "circumcision" raised the discomfort level of everyone around us. (Germans and most Europeans then avoided circumcision and in fact used it as a test for identifying Jews during the Holocaust.) Things Jewish were then commonly noticed and counted. My teacher in the University's German course mentioned one day that there were three Jewish shops in town, no more, no less. This was neither pride nor shame, but something one should know. Why one should know that was not clear to me.

Perhaps the most provocative issue discussed during the year was the debate on whether the twenty-year statute of limitations on murder should be allowed to run its course that year. Of course, during the Third Reich, when prosecution for concentration camp murders was impossible, the prescription period for homicide was "tolled." It could not run when the German government had no choice about prosecuting or not. As soon as the camps were liberated in May 1945, the argument was that the German capacity to prosecute their own murders was reinstated. That implied that the twenty-year period of permissible prosecution would end by

May 1965. This caused a great stir in law enforcement quarters. Many Germans I spoke with in the streets would have been quite happy to see the whole matter laid to rest. *Wir beschmutzen unser eigenes Nest* – We are dirtying our own nest – was the common expression of those who had no interest in further prosecution. After the heated public debates, which I eagerly watched on television, the Bundestag decided to reset the running of the statute so that it would begin in the fall of 1949 when the Federal Republic gained control over its institutions. The crisis was postponed but not for long. In 1969, the legislature extended the period of limitations ten more years and then finally, in 1979, they abolished it. There would be no time limitation on prosecution for murder – and that included murders that had nothing to do with Nazi policies.

The question for lawyers, like myself, was of course: How could they do this? Didn't this violate the prohibition against ex post facto legislation, which is secured in the German *Grundgesetz* (Basic Law) as it is in the American Constitution? The answer is that the prohibition applies only to the core of the offense, the definition of murder. Of course, in the Nuremberg tribunals, the Allies prosecuted for offenses, such as crimes against humanity, that were not defined in statutory form prior to the prosecution. One would think with the alleged abuse at Nuremberg, the Germans would have been very sensitive about prolonging the statute of limitations. But they relied on an important, widely-accepted distinction between substance and form, between defining crimes and defining the rules for prosecuting crimes. I think they were basically right. American courts came to the same conclusion that the statute of limitations is just a matter of procedure and therefore the new legislature can change the law – just the procedural law – to apply to cases already pending in the courts.

These were troubling times. I spent many afternoons exploring Freiburg, wondering what it was like for the Jews who had lived there under Hitler's regime. There had once been a magnificent old synagogue that was burned down on *Krystalnacht* in November 1938. A new university building was built on the location, with a plaque left at the site to remind passersby that the synagogue was once there. I attended many lectures in the new building without knowing that it stood on the place of the old synagogue. I was shocked when I discovered the plaque years later. So far as I knew, the Freiburg faculty had never done anything to honor the Jewish professors who were fired from their jobs in the early stages of the Third Reich. These unredeemed signs of violent anti-Semitism all around me made me feel almost as though I were running a gauntlet – could I get from one side of the town to the other without being attacked? I was haunted by images of Jews being dragged out of their homes and loaded onto trucks. What was I going to do if it actually happened in front of me? As I recall, though I slept all right at night, my days were filled with nightmares. (It should be mentioned, however, that sometime later the Land of Baden-Wuertenberg sponsored the building of a beautiful new synagogue on a valuable piece of land in the center of the city.)

In 1964-65, however, the people I met in the university were not much of a relief from the ghosts that haunted me in the town. In the Max Planck Institute run by Prof. Hans Heinrich Jescheck, there was no one to whom I could confide my feelings about the uncanny post-Nazi mood that swirled all around us. I was not well informed about Jescheck's historical record or for that matter about any of the personalities who were critically important in the university of the 1930s – Martin Heidegger, Edmund Husserl, Erik Wolf. I have had my views about certain people over the years but now that I am put to the test of committing myself to print, I find it more sensible to withdraw to a position of scepticism. I believed, for example, that as a youthful Nazi, Jescheck participated in a hostile march in 1936 to the home of the famous local Jewish philosopher Edmund Husserl. This I now see is pure speculation. Less dubious is Erik Wolf's record as a youthful National Socialist on the faculty. I found his writings in the library and he actually does describe Hitler, more or less, as "blessed for his mission by God." Yet in the 1960s, Erik Wolf was very courteous to me, as was Jescheck, whatever his party history might have been. As students we had a certain obsession about these things. I guess we counted Nazis the way my teacher counted Jewish stores in town. Actually, we counted the Jewish professors too. There were more then than now, largely because the generation trained before the war came back in part, while the Holocaust deprived Germany of successive generations of scientific and academic Jewish personalities.

I did learn one valuable lesson from Jescheck. I attended his lecture on criminal law and one day he was discussing an abstract issue that would never be paid heed in a US law school. I asked him after class whether it was really worthwhile to work on that issue that had so little practical relevance. He replied, correctly, "You never know what will come out of theoretical work."

These simple words of wisdom bore considerable fruit, for I became intensely involved in the internal theoretical debates of the German schools of criminal law. In order to explain what these debates are about, I have to indulge in a few words of legal philosophy. Criminal law overflows with concepts that have a natural appeal to philosophers. Good examples are the concepts of intention, negligence, causation, and human action. The latter term is particularly significant for it is a universal requirement of criminal justice. *No one can be convicted of a crime without engaging in an action in violation of the law.* In this context, I cannot provide you a definition in layman's terms but merely give you an intuitive example. In his satire of the future, *Erewhon*, Samuel Butler imagines a society that punishes having a common cold. You can sense the injustice of this immediately. People get colds involuntarily. They can't do anything to prevent their state of liability. Thus they hardly warrant punishment for sneezing.

The way we would explain this intuition is that sneezing is not a human action. It is an involuntary response, a reaction of the body that can be produced by the right stimuli in the air. Maybe coughs are closer to being actions but if you have noticed, well-trained opera audiences manage to get all their coughing out of their system before the show begins.

In any event, as soon as we leave this world of intuitive examples, and start offering systematic definitions of human action, we are deeply engaged in philosophical inquiry. To say that the question is philosophical is, among other things, to claim that there is an objective truth of the matter, that is, whether a sneeze should be qualified as a human action is not a feeling or a guess or a hunch, it is a matter of fact.

The pursuit of truth does not sit well with the law, which is accustomed to deciding how things should be done, not how they really are. Questions of truth do not lend themselves to trials, with a beginning, two competing sides and a day of decision. The facts of natural science cannot be resolved by legislative fiat. To paraphrase Thomas More in *A Man for All Seasons*: Parliament cannot declare the earth to be flat. If they do pass a law on the matter, it will not make things change. The most they could do would be to prohibit people, subject to their power, from saying or writing that the earth is anything but flat.

This claim about the limits of law applies to the basic philosophical concepts such as intention, negligence, causation, and human action. Alas, Americans have never absorbed this basic truth about law-making. In the influential Model Penal Code, which has served as model of state legislative reform since the 1960s, the American Law Institute laid down authoritative definitions of intention, negligence, causation, and action. You can be sure that they are all transparently wrong and easily subject to philosophical criticism. The German legislature would not dare take a stand on the definitive meaning of these philosophical concepts. These are properly left to scholars who, in the spirit of scientists probing the world, seek to define the basic concepts of the legal culture in a way that can gain the assent of the entire community of lawyers, judges, and scholars.

When we recognize that many concepts in the criminal law

are simply given in the nature of things, then legal theorists have work to do. They have to explain the content of these concepts, find their contours in their inherent meaning. Post-war German legal theorists working on concepts think of themselves, rather grandiosely, as creating a hedge against tyranny. They are right in the sense that they are elaborating a set of concepts binding on both the judiciary and the legislature. This prevents the law from sliding toward extreme limitations on human freedom.

Studying in Germany led me to think that I had something to contribute to these debates about the basic concepts of the legal culture. By getting involved in the crossfire, I began to feel that I was not just an observer of the legal system but a player in the forming of a new academic consensus on the matters that were central to freedom under the law.

My career as a scholar began in these moments in Freiburg when I grasped the ways Europeans think about the relative authority of judges and professors. A turning point occurred in the seminar I took from the great private law scholar, Ernst von Caemmerer. He was the most charismatic teacher in Freiburg. He prowled the aisles, called on students by name, and radiated an energy that invited commitment to the subject. He had been a U-Boat commander during the war. But that was behind him. He was now committed to teaching law. For many years after I started teaching, I consciously imitated von Caemmerer's dramatic performance in the classroom.

In his seminar I did a case study of decisions in a body of law called *positive Vertragsverletzung* – affirmative breach of contract. The Germans thought they could devise a code without mentioning the concept of breach of contract, which is central to the way other countries structure their contract law. You make a contract and then breach it. That makes you liable. That is the simple and nearly universal syllogism of contract law.

The intriguing feature of the original German Civil Code of 1900 is that the authors thought they could do without the concept of breach. That is as bold a claim as creating a legal system with laws but no violations of law. However, as early as 1902, a scholar named Hermann Staub discovered that in certain kinds of cases where people were injured as a result of medical malpractice or other forms of negligence, you could sue in contract only by positing a breach – precisely the concept the Code tried to do without. Of course you could have sued in tort, as you would in many countries for medical malpractice, but there were advantages under German law to suing under a theory of contract. The new doctrine of damages based on contractual breach – though not recognized in the language of the civil code – became a firm part of the law. Anyone who thinks that codes are complete statements of the law need only glance at the innovation of Hermann Staub in 1902.

I learned something more profound than this well-recognized point, that neither the German nor any other civil code is complete and flawless. With the doctrine of "affirmative breach of contract" there was a debate about whether the burden of proof on the issues should lie on one side or the other. The German scholars all came to the same conclusion: the burden should lie, let's say, on the injured party. I did a detailed study of the cases and showed that the scholarly opinions were not substantiated by the cases. Indeed the opposite was true. I read my paper to the seminar, with a certain sense of pride. I had exposed the German scholars as bad scientists: they had misrepresented their sources. Von Caemmerer calmly replied that the cases meant what the scholars said they meant. It would have been like telling Galileo that the movements of the planets are what the Church said they are. No other remark could capture for me the basic ideology of the civil law culture – the legal culture that dominates most of the non-English speaking world. The scholars are not only a source of law, their opinions have a value in their own right, regardless whether they are based on misreporting of the factual background. It would take a decade for my contributions to scholarship to have an impact. In the meantime I made sure that I enjoyed myself.

## *Women in Germany*

My many trips to Freiburg and the Institute have blurred into a single memory. In September of 1964, my first year, my daughter Deborah was born. Taking care of her, of my wife Susan and the house defined most of the rest of the year. In later years, particularly when I was single, I yearned to meet someone, alas without much luck.

The name of the Institute's specialist in English law was Barbara Huber, and she was very hospitable toward me. In her prime she was a very beautiful woman, and I recall admiring her from afar as she went off for dinner or a drink with one or another guest in the Institute. Alas, this perfectly innocent relationship had its complicated side. I had some unverified clues that her father-in-law had been the *Gauleiter* (or party administrative head) in Strasbourg during the war. Her mother was still alive and I met her from time to time at the very pleasant garden parties that Barbara threw in her opulent backyard. It did not occur to me to spend time in Germany without being open to all sorts of friendships, regardless of the past. It seemed silly to run my own moral crusade. I associated with everyone who was friendly with me in the hopes of learning more about the Nazi past – a critical part of my own history. Besides, I found them pleasant people. I enjoyed Germany, and I felt superior to the other foreigners, also often invited to Barbara's parties, who had not mastered the language.

One night after the party, I had an interesting conversation with Mrs. Huber when I was driving her to her home on my side of town. She mentioned that she had a brother in the States.

"How interesting," I said. "Are you in touch?"

"Yes, we are."

"Were you able to communicate during the war?"

I was set back by her response: "*Im Krieg gibt es keine Post*." (Between countries at war, there is no mail.) I use this line often in class to explain to contemporary students the implications of going to war.

Barbara's husband, Konrad, was a genius in his own right. He had his entire record collection of thousands organized by the date of birth of the composer. He could discuss anything with insight, even though his manner reminded one slightly of Dr. Strangelove.

Barbara was estranged from him. It was no surprise to me that she often flirted with me (perhaps it was her form of *Wiedergutmachung* – making things up to the Jews), though I took it all to be perfectly innocent. I cannot forget the time the three of us had dinner with much wine flowing. Her husband left the room. When we were alone Barbara started gently stroking my cheek. I was stunned with no clue how to respond. As the evening wore on, with no plan of action in mind, my only solution was to get drunk – really drunk. I actually vomited when I got back to my room.

If my memories are accurate, my problem was not morality but something else. I valued Barbara's friendship but I could not raise an erotic thought in her direction. I think this was an aspect of the way Germany entered into and shaped my Jewish soul. I was other. She was other. There was no room for erotic space between us, however beautiful she might have been.

In the course of my life, I spent many years in Freiburg, most of the time single and yearning to meet someone. The only Jewish woman I managed to date even for a brief period was a young lawyer I met at the new synagogue in the center of town. I was shocked to find an attractive young Jewish German woman, who actually read the prayer book in Hebrew. She was an intelligent and creative person and I had no good reason for not pursuing her further. She felt no qualms about being German in post-war Germany. If there was a problem, it was "their" problem, not hers. Daniela Breitbart, may you have fared well in life.

Though German women were taboo in my erotic field of vision, this did not deprive Germany of its erotic attraction for me and for the foreign women who met me there. German was the *lingua franca* for theoretical criminal lawyers all over the world. Many attractive foreign academic women were drawn to the Institute in Freiburg, to Frankfurt, to Munich, or to one of the other great centers of the field. One of the more prominent women in my life was a Turk named Oeykue Didim Aydin. She came from a rich family of lawyers that gave her advantages beyond the imagination of ordinary students. She studied a year in Michigan and mastered English and then a year Italy where she learned Italian. She had unlimited funds to do her doctorate in Germany. Despite her teenage fluency in English, our language was German, the language in which we became acquainted in the Institute and in which, for at least a while, we related to each other as friends. We both delighted in showing our mastery of the language. Occasionally we would have arguments about small points of grammar. She often won.

She did some rather remarkable things. Once she cooked me a five-course authentic Turkish meal and served it in her tiny student apartment. She learned some Hebrew on her own and with her family's support, ran for office in Turkey under the banner, "The candidate who speaks Hebrew." But she was also moody. On bad days she would get violent, assaulting me or once trashing my bicycle. She was young, inexperienced and fearful about sex so that was not really an option.

She had frequent trouble with the police. One reason is that she and her sister, also studying in Germany, both had drinking problems. The most serious incident became a cause célèbre in the German-Turkish press. She was moving apartments with her sister when they were both drunk. They called the police because they thought a neighbor was harassing them. When the police arrived, they started arguing with them and Oeykue threw the stiff tube of a vacuum cleaner at them. They took her into custody and according to the Turkish press, beat her up rather badly in the back of the car. As she describes the prison conditions, they were more primitive than what you expect in the anti-Turkish film *Orient Express*. She was put on trial for assaulting the police officers. I attended the trial and wrote an article supporting her against the charges of assaulting the police.

I mention this in order to be honest about my own weaknesses. In my article, published under the title "A Trial in Germany" in Criminal Justice Ethics, I express considerable skepticism about whether she was guilty. The most damning single fact on the side of the prosecution was that they did not bring the vacuum cleaner to trial as evidence. I should have thought if the police did not care enough to bring the instrument of the crime to the trial, the case should have been dismissed. My German friends who read the article regarded me as biased. I could write off this critique to the German authoritarian instinct to believe that the police are likely to be right. The problem is that I also think I was biased. I allowed my friendship with the defendant to color my assessment of the case. You can decide for yourself by reading "A Trial in Germany," available online at Questia.com.

A second friendship in Germany blossomed with a Chinese scholar from Taiwan. Her name was Shue Yue Sheu, as best I can remember the proper transliteration. She called herself Jade in English. We met in 1999 at the Humboldt conference for those who had received Humboldt fellowships to study criminal law in Germany. She was a true believer in the German *Dogmatik* – the name Germans have given to the theory of criminal law. At the time she was a professor of criminal law in Taiwan totally devoted to her work. She had no family, apart from her mother and siblings and no diversions other than the law. She must have spent a lot of time on her clothes because she was probably the most elegantly dressed lady at the conference. She had a fine sense of humor and a playful spirit underlying her compulsive professionalism. We were attending a lecture by a leading figure in German criminal law and she whispered to me, spontaneously in German, "This man is making me old." My sense was that she had to live at high levels of sartorial style in order to be taken seriously as a woman in criminal law. She was eventually promoted to the Supreme Court, where she still serves as a judge.

At one point she invited me to give a tour of lectures in

Taiwan, which was interesting because the Taiwanese scholars are divided in their loyalties among the Japanese, Chinese, and German traditions. Just about every point of view is heard in their discussions. In addition, they have their ancient Taiwanese legal culture, with its distinctive script in Chinese. It is probably the most complicated legal culture I have ever encountered. I suppose for someone like myself who gets along much better with foreign women than with Americans, I had chosen the ideal field. Comparative criminal law was overflowing with lonely people, most of whom were women, looking for companionship. This was not true about the Germans because there were few women in the field who made it past the gauntlet of tests designed to keep them at home with their children. The foreigners were independent spirits. They had to cut themselves off from the controlling influence of their families and venture forth into chance encounters with the world, some of which fortunately included me.

## *The New Code of 1975*

My changing jobs often in the first few years of my teaching (Seattle, Boston, LA – all within four years) made it difficult to find time to travel abroad. Our first daughter Deborah was born during my year in Freiburg, the second, Rebecca, in Seattle in April 1968. My wife Susan had her professional agenda, which was constantly interrupted. Whether I would make a sensible career out of my ties to German law remained an open question. New interests were bourgeoning, primarily in the Soviet Union and Israel – the subjects of our ensuing chapters.

When I expected it least, the German connection became intense once again. In 1975, the West German government replaced its 1871 Criminal Code with a new code reflecting the most sophisticated contemporary theoretical work of 20th century scholars.

In the winter of 1975, Cherif Bassiouni at Chicago-Kent Law, a fine organizer of events and a prodigious writer in the nascent field of international criminal law, called a conference on the new German code. The meeting brought me into contact with Klaus Luederssen from Frankfurt. Luederssen became very enthusiastic about meeting someone who spoke German and who knew something about the German theory of criminal law. He immediately conceived of a plan to introduce me to his closest Frankfurt colleagues in criminal law, Wolfgang Nauke and Winfried Hassemer. I began the summer of 1976 by lecturing there and meeting a very sophisticated group of scholars with whom I have been in contact ever since.

These three scholars made a big difference in my academic development so let me say a word about each of them. Luederssen is the great artist among them. He has an impressionist mind that took him into the far reaches of every field that might be linked up in some way with the law. He writes often for the intellectual German press. His students are among the most successful in the country. The reason I think is that in comparison to someone like Jescheck, he has always been tolerant and supportive of off-beat inquires.

Wolfgang Nauke, now retired for several years, was a rigorous and committed Kantian individualist. He believed firmly in the importance of individual rights – somewhat like Hayek – as a barrier against collectivist thinking. Once on a train ride to a conference, I sat in the same train compartment as Nauke and another colleague. The two of them had a passionate exchange about fundamental principles of law – the kind of debate I had never heard in the US.

Winfried Hassemer, the only Catholic in the group, stood in the middle between the impressionistic and easy-going Luederssen and the committed, disciplined Nauke. Hassemer never tried hard to win friends abroad but many came to study with him in Frankfurt. The Tuesday seminars in the faculty were the event of the week – with graduate students participating from all over the world. It was not surprising with his charm and legal sophistication, Hassemer was chosen to be a judge on the Constitutional Court, where he served as vice president until last year. His greatest moment on the Court, in my mind, was his dissent from a majority decision confirming the conviction of a brother and sister for committing incest. I think every court in the world would have upheld the statute but Hassemer was willing to strike it down as an unconstitutional violation of personal liberty. There is much to learn from his opinion.

My Frankfurt colleagues invited me back as visiting professor in the fall of 1980, but this is getting ahead of our story.

I used the return visit to Germany in 1976 to travel around the country to meet the leading people in the field. I had already begun reading the writings of Albin Eser in Tuebingen. I don't think he knew much about me but I had a good sense for the style of his work. I decided to take the train to Tuebingen and then look him up. I called him from the train station. Eser answered and the following conversation ensued.

"Who is this?"

"This is one of your fans from the United States. I have read a lot of your work and I would like to meet you. I am downtown at the train station."

"Are you traveling around Germany?"

"Yes."

"When is your next appointment?"

"In about four or five days."

The phone seemed to drop on the other end. But the voice eventually came back on and invited me to come and stay for a few days. They had an extra room and it would, he said, "be no trouble at all." They came to pick me up at the train station and in the meantime I had bought a bouquet of red roses for Mrs. Eser. Little did I know that red roses are a symbol of unconfessed love reserved for a very special woman. Gerda Eser, whom I met for the first time, took it all in her stride.

The five days with the Esers became an intense seminar in the theory of the criminal law. Albin invited various colleagues over and together we drank from his wine cellar until the wee hours of the morning. He had to get up to teach, so he frequently excused himself early. But the rest of us drank as though we were about to find the ultimate truths of criminal responsibility. The *chutzpa* on my side was not to be underestimated, but nor was the generosity and flexibility of my German hosts.

The summer of 1976 proved to be the beginning of a very intensive period of interchange with my German colleagues. I applied for and received a grant from the German Marshall Fund, which enabled me to attend regular meetings of their Alternative Group for the Reform of Criminal Procedure. I flew from Los Angeles to exotic spots in Germany and usually spent the first day falling asleep during the discussions, but all in all, I had a wonderful time at these mini-conferences that generally lasted 4-5 days. There was plenty of time for social life and bonding with my colleagues. One of the clever things that Germans do when they hold conferences is that they always reserve a half day for an *Ausflug* – a hike or some other expedition into the countryside. Admittedly, the analysis of criminal procedure was a little over my head, but I was absorbing the German style of argument into my way of thinking.

With our celebration and our easy social relations, we forgot not only the aftermath of the Holocaust but the political conflicts that made Germany the hottest spot in the cold war of the 1970s. One of these conflicts soon came to the center of my life.

## *The Tiede Case*

The biggest source of tension in the first 25 years after the collapse of Germany was division among the three parts of the former Reich. East Germans risked their lives to escape into the West. Border guards shot them and sometimes killed them. This was a situation overflowing with problems for criminal lawyers.

One very enterprising East German named Detlef Tiede triggered a criminal case that tested the foundations of peace among the three parts of Germany. In the summer of 1978, the young Tiede was on vacation in Gdansk, now in Poland, with his girlfriend, Ingrid Ruske, and her daughter. He decided that he had enough of life in the DDR. He did not fear specific acts of violence or torture, but the very idea of being imprisoned by the wall was too much for him, and apparently as well for his girlfriend Ingrid. They conceived a plan for highjacking a plane of the Polish Lot airline headed back to Berlin. Ingrid's twelve-year-old daughter had a plastic toy pistol. They could easily sneak that past security, which was lighter in those casual pre-9/11 days. Once on board, Tiede grabbed the pistol and pushed it into the back of the head of one of the stewardesses, threatening to shoot if she did not comply and direct the pilot to land the plane in the American sector of Berlin, Tempelhof Airport. The pilot complied.

The de facto rules of the four-power occupation permitted the passengers on the plane to flee immediately and claim asylum. Of course, 20-odd passengers ran for freedom immediately. But Tiede and Ruske were arrested. The problem was what would be done with them. It was hard to accuse them of a crime in West Germany. They were heroes who had fled the dictatorial DDR. Yet it was hard to deny that they had committed a serious crime. They hijacked an airplane. After 9/11 their crime would have been looked upon with particular gravity. How could the West Germans be sure they had no hostile purposes? The Western authorities did not consider shooting down the plane. At the same time, German legal officials could not simply let both Tiede and Ruske go. Though Ingrid and her daughter would be released relatively quickly for humanitarian reasons, Tiede had to stand trial. A serious crime was committed and the precedent of letting him go would be dangerous to the future of aviation in the region.

Under the occupation arrangement between Germany and the United States, the Americans were entitled to establish a United States Court in Berlin. This seemed like the better solution for the trial of Tiede. The Americans took custody over the hijacker with the implicit permission of the Germans who did not want to try him anyway. The State Department was in charge of the occupation of Berlin and it was their decision whether to go forward and set up a special federal court in Berlin. They did so and appointed a federal judge from New Jersey, Herbert Stern, to preside.

The new US Court for Berlin had a case but no one knew exactly what they would do with it and what law they would apply. The first decision was obvious: German law would apply to the highjacking because it was committed, in part, over German territory. General Eisenhower had endorsed the territorial principle for American courts sitting in Berlin so this point was not subject to much controversy. The more difficult question was which procedural law would apply. Would the US Constitution apply? It seems like a far fetched question now, particularly in light of nine solid years of the Bush and Obama administrations' campaign to treat Guantanamo Bay as beyond the reach of the Constitution. In 1978, the question was taken very seriously. If the government exercised power in Berlin, then arguably it must be governed by the Constitution.

A complicating factor was that the US Court was not a real court established under Article III of the Constitution. It was a so-called Article II Court, an executive court acting under the authority of the State Department and the Ambassador. The State Department thought they could run the court as their own agency and that the judge would take orders from them. Once the judge was appointed, however, they confronted a new reality: a judge would act like a judge no matter how he or she was appointed.

No matter which court he runs, a judge is going to think of himself as sovereign in the courtroom. It is almost impossible to convince a federal judge – whatever the formal nature of the court – that the defendant has only those rights granted to him by the State Department. The claim itself is an insult to the judicial function and its cherished sense of independence. The judge's opinion on these issues reeks with anger and insult. Note this exchange between the judge and André Surena, who was the Legal Advisor to the US Mission in Berlin:

Judge: Must the Court take the directives of the Secretary

of State?

Surena: The Court cannot go beyond whatever restrictions the Department of State places upon the Court.

Judge: How will I know when you are arguing to me and when you are telling me on the other hand? So if I understand your position correctly, I have nothing to decide. I have only to obey.

The last line was decisive. The idea of a court that just takes orders is a contradiction in itself. The upshot of this exchange was that the judge ruled that the US Constitution applied in West Berlin and the defendant had all the rights that a defendant in a US court would have. The most critical of these was a right to a jury trial.

This is a very significant decision in and of itself. The case should be remembered and cultivated for the judge's heroic stand in the face of the people who appointed him. Unfortunately it was not picked up by the literature and has not received the commentary and praise it deserves.

Therefore, I wish to highlight the trial of Detlef Tiede as one of the great jurisprudential breakthroughs of its time. May it still come to play in controversies about the application of the Constitution to Guantanamo and other American prison camps for foreigners abroad.

The trial was scheduled to begin in the summer of 1979. There were technical problems putting together a jury of West Berliners. The selection of the jury implied that the trial would have to be conducted in both languages. This was not a serious problem. The lawyers all spoke English and a team of translators was installed that made a bilingual trial easy and comfortable. I never knew much about the budget for the trial. Perhaps the State Department could have pulled the strings but after Judge Stern's courageous decision I doubt if they dared.

The biggest problem for the Americans, believe it or not, was understanding the applicable German criminal law. The defense team, led by top-flight Washington lawyer Judah Best, interviewed some German professors of criminal law about the applicable law. They could not understand what the Germans were talking about. The problem was not language but a conceptual disconnect. The professors conveyed the simple point that intimidating the plane's crew with a plastic pistol constituted highjacking. But they had little imagination about possible defenses. The challenge of Judah Best was to bring to bear the context of a desperate East Berliner doing what he had to do to seek his freedom. The public sentiment in favor of Tiede had to find some expression in the law.

This is where I came in. Judah Best decided that trying to communicate with English-speaking German lawyers was hopeless. He made a decision for which I have great respect. He decided that he had to find an American who understood the German theory of criminal law. Judah Best conducted a nation-wide search and he landed on the doorstep of the one person in the country who, for no particularly good reason except love of the subject, knew the German system of criminal law. There is a message in this someplace – I think it is that if you do something totally impractical, it is unlikely that other people will follow you. You will be all alone out there. This has certain advantages. If the odd chance that the impractical art turns practical for just a moment, you will be the person of the moment (maybe).

A long limo rolled up in front of my house in Santa Monica in the spring of 1979. Judah Best stepped out, alone. He came in and sat with me in my back office, the corner room furthest from the street. All I had there was a door-size desk, which I had made out of two doors (one sliced in half and serving as the legs for the desk), a couple of chairs, and a red-flowered sofa, which I picked up at a garage sale for $50.00. Judah Best must have been comfortable in this home-crafted room. He relaxed. We spoke for a few minutes, he offered me the job, and I was on a plane a week later for Berlin.

My job was officially to be an expert witness for the defense. They were paying me, so there was nothing wrong with leaning sentimentally toward the defense. When I boarded the plane, I had no idea how we were going to win the case. I would wait, listen, and think.

Our living arrangements in Berlin were superb. All the lawyers, the judge, and the judge' clerk stayed in one of the luxury hotels in town, the Kempinsky. We sat at separate tables at breakfast but we quickly got to know each other. It turned out that the judge's chief clerk – whose function was much like mine – was Thomas Weigend, an assistant to Professor Jescheck then specializing in American law at the Max Planck Institute in Freiburg. We had known each other casually for years and there is no doubt that with respect to the German and English languages, and German and American law, he was very much my equal. I had published my first major book on comparative criminal law the year before and Weigend had written a competent and positive review of the book. Yet I was not worried about Weigend as an adversary, however talented he may have been. The German system trains people to think conventionally – whenever possible in normal channels. The only thing that was going to win this case was an argument totally outside the box. I had not yet figured out what it was.

## *The Abortion Argument in Germany*

The clue to Tiede's defense lay in the curious way that the solution to the abortion problem has evolved in Germany. Solving the abortion problem is one of the most difficult questions that every Western democracy has faced. The essential problem is that it pits innocent life against innocent life and there is no easy justification for a court to intervene on the side either of the fetus or of the mother. As of 1927, the German code adopted the Catholic position and strictly prohibited all abortions. The only possible exception was that the mother herself could be excused for choosing the abortion if her life was in danger. But the doctors who performed the abortion acted illegally. They had no statutory defense to their violation.

In what appeared to be an easy case for conviction, the court acquitted the doctors, but the prosecution appealed to reverse the acquittal and the decision to punish the doctors (this is possible in Germany and in many countries). The appellate court reversed and sent the case back for trial. Once again the judge dismissed the charges. It was clear that public sentiment was at odds with the strict anti-abortion law. Once again the prosecution appealed, the appellate court reversed and this time the prosecution's appeal went to the Supreme Court. In hearing the appeal, the Supreme Court engaged in a radical redefinition of the law.

Most people think that civil law systems – like Germany, France, and Italy – are strictly governed by codes. The codes are like recipes that prescribe what must be done in every case. This is not true, and certainly not in Germany. Earlier I mentioned the modification of the civil code by the addition of the doctrine of affirmative breach of contract. What the German Supreme Court did with the abortion law was much more radical. It began its reasoning on the premise that abortion could be punishable only if it was "unlawful." You would think that the statute would decide once and for all whether the abortion was unlawful. It is a simple proposition. The statute prohibits all abortion, therefore it is unlawful for doctors to do it.

But as the Supreme Court reasoned, it was not that simple. We ultimately must decide whether abortion is contrary to the law writ large, and the law in this broader sense contains principles and values that are not written in the Code. One of these principles, they argued, is called: acting for the sake of the lesser evil. This is a very familiar argument in moral philosophy. When two goods – life against life – collide, the correct thing is to choose the lesser evil, also called the greater good. If the life of the mother is a greater good than the life of the fetus, then the lesser evil is to sacrifice the fetus.

But how can the life of the fetus be compared with the life of the mother? This has taxed many moral philosophers. Should it matter how old the mother is, what her personal talents are, whether the fetus is perfectly formed? You can imagine an infinite variety of cases. An essential assumption to those who seek a relatively simple solution to the problem is to regard the fetus as a developing human being. The embryo, arguably, has a lower moral status in its first minute of life than the fetus has at three months. When the heart starts beating, it has even greater moral status. When the fetus can live on its own, separated from the mother, it has nearly complete human status. This is the approach of the United States Supreme Court in the famous case of Roe v. Wade (1972). It is the approach of any court that seeks an alternative to the Catholic position that the embryo is equivalent to a human life from the moment of conception.

The progressive development of the fetus leads to a form of thinking that has become commonplace in legal systems around the world. It is called "balancing competing interests." In German: *Gueterabwaegung.* This is the method for deciding which is the greater good or the lesser evil. The basic idea is that the conflicting parties have interests, these interests have weights, and the weights are subject to comparison and balancing. Specifically, in the 1927 Abortion Case, the court developed the idea that abortion would not be wrongful unless it represented a violation of the more important interest at stake. Thus, if the doctor intervened to save the life of the fetus when the mother's interests outweighed the interest of the young fetus, the action would not be wrongful and therefore not criminal.

The ramifications of the 1927 decision extend throughout the legal system. Whenever a serious risk of harm and the principle of lesser evils imply that the violation of the statutory law is permissible, the defendant cannot be convicted. This is called the general principle of necessity, and in particular, the extra-statutory principle of necessity because in 1927 it was not defined or regulated by any statute. The phrase "extra-statutory necessity" took on a doctrinal life of its own. It was adopted into Spanish and Latin American law and other systems that are heavily influenced by German theory.

We can begin to see how this principle of "extra-statutory necessity" became applicable in the 1979 highjacking case. The statute clearly and explicitly prohibits highjacking but perhaps there is a balancing of interests that makes the highjacking justifiable under certain circumstances. After all, Detlef Tiede was arguably desperate not to return to life in the DDR. There was no impending risk of arrest or torture but he "felt" desperate. This is the same sense of distress that led many men and women to scale the wall and take their chances of being shot as they swam across the channel separating the two Germanys.

American federal judges do not have much familiarity with necessity arguments. There is nothing in federal jurisprudence that comes close to the 1927 Abortion Case. The Model Penal Code recognizes a general principle of lesser evils as a justification but it is badly drafted and the federal courts pay little attention to it. Thus these arguments were relatively new to Judge Stern. I presented the argument in court, more as an advocate than an expert witness. Tiede was justified in using force to take the airplane because that was the only way for him to escape the burdens of life in the DDR. We did not go into many details about these "burdens" because our audience was, after all, a jury of sympathetic West Berliners.

One day I walked out in front of Tempelhof Airport and noticed that Soviet troops were marching back and forth in front of our courtroom. They had a right to do this. But I doubt if anyone in the Soviet Embassy was following the trial very closely. They did not realize that we were developing an argument that justified highjacking an airplane as an evil less egregious than the way of life promoted by the Communist governments.

The argument of necessity obviously worked. The prosecution dismissed the charges against Ingrid Ruske and following the judge's instructions on necessity, the jury acquitted Tiede of all counts but one concerning the highjacking. And on that count, Stern sentenced him to time served; Tiede had been in custody for eight months pending trial. He walked out of court a free man.

That night I took the subway across to the Eastern sector of Berlin and boarded the overnight train from Berlin to Budapest. As soon as I had a chance to relax in my compartment, I experienced a sense of shock and burst out loud, "My God, what have I done?" I have just gotten a man off for highjacking an airplane. There were certainly good arguments against my claim of necessity but they were not heard forcefully in court. For one thing, necessity is not applicable against what is called a "lasting and ongoing danger." There was nothing about Tiede's situation that made him fear an imminent risk of harm. He faced the gruesome conditions that applied to all DDR citizens. If he was justified, then so would be anyone who used force to escape. Perhaps those were the sentiments of the times, but they were hardly supported by the doctrine of necessity first applied in the 1927 Abortion Case.

My feelings of unease about having helped Tiede escape punishment for highjacking is a typical sentiment for lawyers who are effective because they have mastered both sides of the case. When you win, you feel that you have cheated the other side. You know that if you were the other side, you could have won as well. This was not the last time I would feel this particular sense of discomfort, but I admit I enjoyed getting used to it.

## *The New Absolutism*

I always teach the 1927 Abortion Case in my classes on comparative law because, to my mind, it represents the best of the creative method of the civil law system. Since the war and the adoption of the German *Grundgesetz* (Basic Law) in 1949 there has been a gradual shift away from balancing interests in favor of an absolutist commitment to human life and to a new value enshrined in Article 1 of the Basic Law: human dignity (*Menschenwuerde*) as an absolute value. The first obvious shift has been in the field of abortion itself. The new attitude is based on the principle "everyone has a right to life" as stated in Article 2 of the Basic Law. This right to life applies to fetuses. Thus we are back to the Catholic position in which two absolutes collide without room for give and take. In the first decision, in 1975, the Court went so far as to argue that the post-war liberal abortion law was unconstitutional because it did not sufficiently protect the life of the fetus. Parliament was under a duty to enact a new law and if they did not do it, the Court would legislate, temporarily, in its place. This is a form of judicial activism we have never seen in the United States, that is, the courts instructing the legislature to punish when the latter chooses not to.

Since the killing of the fetus was always wrong, the Court developed a new jurisprudence of "indications" that would make some abortions permissible without saying they were right or wrong. And then they added a requirement of the pregnant woman's consultation with a doctor to clarify, supposedly, whether she was doing what was in her best interest. Whatever the current compromise, the Court has sought to maintain the idea that the fetus has an absolute right to life under German Basic Law.

In recent years, the Court has gone even further in protecting the right to life. This widely recognized right – coupled with the uniquely German guarantee of human dignity in Article 1 of the Basic Law – led to a decision in 2006 that surprised the world. In the wake of 9/11, the German Parliament passed a law that enabled the military forces to shoot down hijacked airplanes headed toward civilian population centers. The point was obvious. If another 9/11 is in the making, we should do what we can to prevent it. It would seem to be obvious that the military has the authority to protect the country against aggressive attacks. I believe this would be taken for granted in the United States, where the president has authority to defend the country from foreign aggression and the military serves under presidential command. No legislative authorization should be necessary, but the German Parliament thought they should have a statute in place before the risk materialized.

Hard to believe but the German High Court rejected the principle of balancing competing interests when it came to the conflict between innocent victims and aggressive terrorists. There might be innocent people on board a hijacked airliner, they reasoned. They have a right to life. Their dignity must be protected. How can they be sacrificed just to defend the country? The Court admitted that if the plane consisted entirely of hijackers it could be shot down. But the lives of innocent passengers could not be converted into disposable "objects" – as the mere means to an end. In reaching this decision the Court relied heavily on the post-war influence of Immanuel Kant's philosophy of moral absolutes.

In a shift of jurisprudence of this magnitude, from balancing interests for the sake of the net social good in 1927 to recognizing the inviolable right to life and human dignity, one can only sense that German guilt must have played a part. Establishing a *Rechtsstaat* – a state based on the rule of law – is no easy achievement after 12 years of one of most murderous regimes in history.

But guilt has its excesses. Admittedly, the sentiment of guilt led to reparations to the Jews and this enabled the reestablishment of diplomatic relations between Germany and Israel. Even today Germany feels a special responsibility to stand with Israel in the face of general hostility in the United Nations. At the same time, German guilt merged in an unfortunate way with the faith of the Catholic Church, which wields great influence over nearly half of its population. The "right to life" is taken to excesses not found in other Western democracies. Perhaps some Catholic countries are as rigorous when it comes to scientific research and in vitro fertilization where it appears that something like the termination of an incipient life might occur.

But the wages of guilt have also generated the decision of 2006 that the German authorities cannot shoot down an airliner headed for a mass massacre. If the US Congress adopted a statute like the German statute, it surely would not be declared unconstitutional because it permitted the government to sacrifice the lives of innocent people. Deliberately failing to shoot down a hijacked plane endangering your own civil population would be grounds, in my opinion, for impeaching the president. His or her duty is to protect the civil population against external aggression. In any wartime action, civilians are bound to die.

By following these developments in German legal thought, we have strayed a long way from my subject, which is my life in the German language. Yet it is not an accident that Kant and Hegel wrote in German. And it is not an accident that I have been particularly attracted to German philosophy, which I read in the original. The German language lends itself to abstract philosophical propositions. It has a precise vocabulary for expressing moral absolutes. When you are speaking German, you can sometimes take these abstractions to be more real than the ground under your feet.

Chapter Three

# My First Mission: Russian

As I signed up for Russian in my second year at Cornell, I knew I was continuing a pattern that had begun with German in high school. I was drawn to the language of the enemy. Human contact with the enemy carries a dimension of drama and excitement missing, most of all, in the study of the tourist languages – Spanish, Italian, etc. The year was 1957, just before Sputnik. My opting for Russian was a precocious choice to get myself, somehow, into the midst of the cold war.

The joke at the time was that pessimists studied Chinese; optimists, Russian. I suppose the assumption was that if the Chinese ended up the rulers of the world, life would be absolutely unbearable; under the Russians, it would only be relatively unbearable. We thought of the Russians as enemies, but still part of our civilization. The Chinese were true aliens. As things have turned out, the joke had it backwards. Except for civil liberty issues, China is a marvelous place to visit and even to live – if you have enough money. There is very little attractive and interesting about post-Communist Russia.

In those days leading up to Sputnik, I dreamt of some kind of mission to Communist Russia. I did everything possible to flout my sympathy for the language and the people. I had a huge map of the USSR, in Russian, stretched across my bedroom wall.

I dreamt of spending nine days on the train from Vladivostok to Moscow. A few friends and I greeted each other by first names and patronymics. I was always and still am called Georgij Nikolaevich, because my father's name was Miklós or Nikolas in Russian.

My first year in Russian was not very impressive or well-organized. There was an oppressive amount of grammar to be learned. Russian has some grammatical twists that make it particularly difficult to master. It has the German and Latin system of three genders, declined in six cases, two more than in German, but this is just a variation on a theme. The structure of the verbs is a feast of technicalities so intertwined that it tests the capacities of even those adept at grammar. The problem begins with the absence of the conventional tense system. German and English – and the Romance languages with some variations – all have the same verb structures – past, present, future, past perfect, present perfect, and future perfect. If these six categories take hold in your mind, you can orient yourself well in the language.

Russian has a different take on time. The critical distinction is between continuing or repeated conduct and finite time-bound action. These are called, respectively, the imperfect and perfect aspects of the verb. Verbs come in pairs, one in the imperfect and the other in the perfect form. Frequently they have no visual similarity.

The translation of a simple phrase like "Can I help you?" becomes complicated. Do I mean that I wanted to help you on one occasion, say carrying a large package? Or do I mean I want to tutor you in your studies every day for an indefinite period?

This is a relatively simple case. In my experience, I have found that the right verb to use depends not so much on logic but on usage. You just have to listen to how people speak and imitate them. This is particularly true in the snake pit called verbs of motion. When you are going, traveling, carrying, bringing, the verb forms multiply out of control. I have learned, contrary to my rule-loving instincts, to follow paradigms in these areas. If you know that you should use one phrase when you are about to leave for a trip (*oo-ezhaiu*, for example) you must use it whether it makes grammatical sense or not.

As with most languages, you can learn to talk around the minefield of grammatical technicalities. You need a few paradigms that come in handy in daily use but you do not need to keep your interlocutor waiting while you are trying to figure out the correct form.

The second year course is when we learned Russian. There were six of us, meeting every day at the same hour with a strict disciplinarian, an older Russian woman from Kiev. She was not a scholar of Russian but she knew how to teach. We used the US military system of memorizing prescribed sentences and using those sentences over and over again in class. Soon we found ourselves using those sentence and variations on them when we would meet on campus. The class was more like a seminary than a course of instruction. We were all committed from day one. As things turned out, at least four of the six in the class made professional careers based on our knowledge of Russian. There are two whose names I do not remember. Of the other three, one became head of the Woodrow Wilson School in Princeton and then president of Northwestern University. Another became a professor of Russian studies in a small college in New York. A third moved to Jerusalem and taught Russian at the Hebrew University.

At the end of the year I had a rare meeting with Vladimir Nabokov who then taught literature at Cornell. He was then writing *Lolita* and riding the busses in Ithaca in order to pick up teenage lingo. He wanted his next project to be his translation of Pushkin's *Eugene Onegin.* To do this he wanted to offer a seminar the following year on Pushkin. He wanted us to take the class. One of my great regrets is that I was not able to return to Cornell to be there and witness the great Nabokov at work. My father became ill in Los Angeles and I had to stay nearby.

Whether I could put my Russian to a practical end remained to be seen. I went to law school and tried there to take advantage of my Russian with Professor Rheinstein, whom I mentioned in my memoir of German. In order to get closer to him, I suggested I do an independent study for him on some aspect of Soviet law. Soviet law was not taught at Chicago, and if it were, I probably would not have been interested (later I will explain the kind of work that the US Sovietologists did in those years). I picked a subject that suggested something unique and attractive about the Soviet system – namely the comrades' courts, the informal neighborhood courts that maintained discipline in apartment buildings and clamped down on deviant behavior. There were lots of articles written about them in the Soviet journals. I spent weeks in the Chicago and Northwestern libraries reading all the journals, taking notes, and summarizing my findings. When I presented the paper to Prof. Rheinstein, he responded with a low grade. I was shocked because I thought I was so unusual that I could do the research in Russian. When I asked him about it, he replied, famously, "Any hack in the State Department could have written that." This was a significant moment in my academic education. A Russian immigrant later helped me to conceptualize Rheinstein's attitude. When I criticized her in the language Rheinstein applied to me, she said, "Oh. I see I need more 'academism' in my work." I understood her to mean that research must include a spark of originality, a critical perspective. It is not enough to report on what is going on.

In addition to the point about academia he taught me, my working for Rheinstein paid off. I learned to consume Russian journals and newspapers at a near-fluent pace, and Rheinstein knew me well enough to invite me to join his graduate program in German law, one year with him in Chicago, and one year in Freiburg.

Learning Russian is not something you can do in a few years. You must keep it up all the time by finding tutors, by finding people you can speak to in the language and by reading newspapers and literature (admittedly I have not done enough of the latter). As I was waiting for my mission, I was fortunate in finding people who would speak Russian with me. I would visit them once for a week for a conversation over tea, sometimes paying them for tutoring, sometimes not. My first wife Susan's Aunt Bobbie (Barbara, I presume), a passionate, almost violent woman – the only wild spirit in a family of German Jews – grew up speaking Russian in her family. She found in me a kindred spirit – another misfit in the family – and she was more than delighted to meet with me on a regular basis to speak what we took to be the language of Romantics. Then later in Seattle, when I was teaching at the age of 26, I found an old emigree who cheerfully tutored me once a week. Thinking about these two older women, I was prepared to conclude that my experience of learning Russian in those post-university days consisted in conversations with mature ladies, but then I thought of Alya.

She was by far the most intriguing and dangerous encounter I ever had with the Russian language. Alya was my second tutor in Seattle and quickly became my friend. As I recall her, she was slim and brainy looking, simple in dress, with an intense regard that kept your focus on her. She was a professional linguist, having completed her doctorate under Roman Jakobson and other leaders in the field at Harvard. I discovered something with Alya that probably accounts for my fascination with languages. When speaking a foreign language – particularly a Romantic one like Russian – you very quickly enter a magic circle from which the surrounding environment is excluded. Alya and I felt an enormous attraction to each other, no doubt engendered by our high octane linguistic orbiting. But I was an honorable married man, and however strongly tempted, I could not descend from the abstract reaches of language to the yearnings of the flesh. My behavior toward her sometimes resembled a stray dog wandering the streets looking for an encounter, and I knew that would be beyond my limits. Since then Alya has lain suspended deeply in the recesses of my mind, a painful reminder of having been much too honest a man. She was forgotten until the blessings of writing this memoir brought her alive for me.

## *Hearing the Call*

In the last week of December 1970, in the course of my first trip to Israel when I was riding in a cab north on the coastal highway, I heard, we all heard, a high-pitched siren. The driver stopped the car and got out and stood at attention. The passengers followed suit. Then we saw that all the other drivers had also stopped and they and their riders were also standing on the pavement. I had never witnessed anything like it.

I asked around. People told me that this was a nationwide protest against the death sentence against two Jews – Mark Dymshitz and Eduard Kuznetzov – handed down by a court in Leningrad. They were caught trying to hijack an airplane, I was told. The death sentence for an attempted highjacking! Unbelievable, I thought. I did not know it then but my mission was trying to reach me. It would take a few more years for my path to intersect with my mission.

The details of the Leningrad trial became more clear to me as I read the newspapers in the ensuing days. On June 15 of the same year, the police stopped a group of people, mostly Jews, headed toward the tarmac of a small airport in Smolny near Leningrad. The police alleged that the group had a plan to hijack the plane and fly it safely to Sweden, where they would seek asylum. The police obviously had an informer in the group because nothing in the behavior of the Jews indicated a clear intention to seize the airplane by force. So far as I could tell, they had no weapons on them.

The Leningrad Municipal Court held a trial on December 15, 1970, just as I was preparing for my first trip to Israel. As the Soviet authorities viewed the case, this was not a case of a dozen or so conspirators. This was the tip of a large movement of Soviet Jews to leave the USSR and settle in Israel, the US, Canada, or wherever they pleased. The authorities decided to react with maximum severity and therefore they sentenced two of the leaders to death. Israel responded with the same gravity. This became a major test of wills between the USSR and Israel and the West in general. The overreaction of imposing the death penalty enabled the Israeli government to mount a worldwide drive of sympathy for Soviet Jews "imprisoned" in their own land.

The amazing thing is that it worked. The Soviet court reversed the death penalty and imposed a sentence of 15 years, the maximum sentence short of death permitted under Soviet law. Of course, the conspirators remained in jail. Their convictions were upheld.

I was interested in doing something to help out but I did not know what I could do as an academic in California. But soon thereafter the mission found its man. In the year 1973-74 I was asked to serve as a visiting professor at the Harvard Law School. I had known Alan Dershowitz from previous interactions in the field of criminal law. Just at that moment as I was sitting in an office down the hall from Alan and preparing my classes, a group of New York lawyers decided to raise funds in order to field a major legal intervention on behalf of Soviet Jews seeking to emigrate.

The problem was not just the group serving their sentence as the result of the First Leningrad trial, but there was also a second Leningrad trial and other trials all around the country. And beyond the field of those in jail, there was the vast number of Jews who tried to get exit permits and were then fired from their jobs. They were called the "*otkazniki*," literally "refuseniks." Those in jail were called the "prisoners of Zion." They became pawns in the cold war.

Today, near the Inbal Hotel in Jerusalem, there is a plaque in honor of Senator Henry Jackson. I would imagine that virtually no Israelis and few visiting Americans under the age of 40 have a clue who he was. In fact he was a right-wing Democratic senator from the state of Washington – not somebody liberal Jews would ordinarily support. But because of his close emotional ties to Soviet Jews, he sponsored a trade bill that punished the Soviets for restricting emigration – the Jackson/Vanik amendment – and thus he became a hero in Israel. Left-wing activists did not really want support from cold-war mongers, but in fact the politics of Israel and the Soviet Union produced paradoxical alliances. Witness the support socialist Zionists are willing to accept today from the American evangelical movement.

From the Soviet point of view, the issue was whether they would have enough time to change the habits of a stable population in order to make communism work in their country. If the West succeeded in inducing their educated people to leave for the sake of better jobs and a wealthier lifestyle, the Soviet alternative, in their opinion, would not have a chance.

The lawyers wanted to find a way to help all the Jews to leave who wanted to, but this was not a problem that lent itself to a compelling argument in legal terms. The Soviets had their emigration rules and though there might have been various international norms applicable to the situation, in the final analysis, the sovereign countries of the world retain the authority to regulate immigration and emigration. The prisoners in jail were another story. If they were convicted under an abuse of power, under a violation of Soviet law itself, the regime was vulnerable to serious embarrassment on the stage of world politics.

One of the curious things about legal systems is that when a government publishes a set of laws and regulations, they are taken at their word. They cannot say: these laws were just a bluff, actually we do whatever we want to do. It is not clear why their integrity prevents them from conceding that their legal system is a charade. Deep in the recesses of the Western mind, we hold to the view that the law consists in a set of sincere promises of the regime to abide by the rules it declares to be applicable.

When the New York lawyers first established the project, they had no idea what they would find. They decided to start by signing up General Telford Taylor who had been chief American prosecutor in Nuremberg and who had a close personal association with the Soviet chief prosecutor, now Procurator General in the USSR, Roman Rudenko. Taylor could not simply go to Rudenko and say "Let Moses' people go!" He needed something to back up an argument that the imprisonments were unjust attacks against Soviet Jews as a whole. After all, if the Leningrad conspirators and others convicted of crimes were really guilty and properly tried under Soviet law, where was the beef?

Dershowitz had been a student of Taylor's at Yale. They were on good terms and Alan was already becoming a key legal figure in the Eastern Jewish establishment. Taylor and Dershowitz became a team, supported by the fund-raising effort in New York. They needed an expert on Soviet law to advise them on the legality of the trials.

At the time there were three major experts on Soviet law teaching in American law schools – John Hazard at Columbia, Leon Lipson at Yale, and Harold Berman at Harvard. It would have been natural for Dershowitz to invite Berman to join the team as their expert. But the problem of Soviet studies in the 1970s was that the academic experts were resolved to stay out of politics. Otherwise they would lose their contacts in the USSR and they would not even be able to get visas to enter the country. The team had to settle for a younger person who did not care that much whether he would succeed as a Soviet specialist. (Lipson did join the group in its final stages.) Dershowitz knew that one of his buddies – working right down the hall – had studied Russian and could do the job.

But there was still a hurdle. Taylor wanted to make sure I was qualified. We held a meeting with one of the prisoner's family members in New York. When we were all seated, Taylor turned to me and said, "O.K. interview her in Russian." I managed to pull it off, and the interviewee was kind enough not to correct me, if I made any mistakes. Apparently this part of the job was the most important. Taylor was willing to take my legal qualifications at face value.

It turned out to be a very enriching experience. Not only were there many trips to Israel and the Soviet Union, but I was able to put my knowledge of Russian and comparative law to valuable use.

Taylor and I took our first trip to Israel in December 1973. Our purpose was to interview the family members of the prisoners in order to learn more about the trials and, hopefully, to find a factual basis for alleging violations of Soviet law. We stayed initially at the Park Plaza Hotel in Tel Aviv and then later at the Kings Hotel at the corner of King George and Rambam Streets in Jerusalem.

Soon after our arrival we had dinner with Yoram Dinstein, a leading professor of international law in Tel Aviv, very supportive of our effort. He took me aside at the dinner and asked me, "Is he Jewish? Is he Jewish?" I thought this was very funny. Of course, Taylor – who looked like a general straight from central casting – was not Jewish. He was simply a decent man who wanted to do the right thing. Yoram provided critical support and became fond of the project. Years later I heard him say that the Taylor project was one of the few run by academics that actually produced results.

A few days after we arrived, Dershowitz's friend Jeannie Baker, a lawyer from Boston, showed up at our hotel. We soon figured out she was Alan's friend, who for some reason was not to be known publicly as his traveling companion. When he took a piece of meat from her plate, I announced, "Until now I had my suspicions, now I know for sure!" We all had a good laugh about that. We bonded together very quickly, which was critical for the eventual progress of our mission.

Prior to this trip to Israel, we had not accomplished anything. The first task was to find out what happened at the trials. The preparation for our visit – presumably under Dinstein's charge – was excellent. We had several days of interviews lined up. We talked to people who had been at the trials or whose family members were convicted.

A pattern quickly appeared in the testimonies we heard. Apart from the highjacking-related trials, there were a couple of basic charges that Rudenko's procuracy used to prosecute the Jewish activists. The two most common charges were based on the possession of anti-Soviet literature and participation in an anti-Soviet organization. Neither of these would be crimes in the United States, first because of the principle of free speech, and second because of the principle that membership per se cannot constitute a crime in the US (more about that principle later in the chapter on English and the discussion of the Hamdan case). And the acts called treason in the First Leningrad trial would not be considered treason in the US either. This kind of comparative argument is interesting for me personally, but it is of no value in trying to argue with the Soviets.

The emphasis had to be on the internal violation of Soviet law – not on a comparison of their law with ours. What they define as crime is their own business. But in the mysterious ways of the law, which they are bound by, they must follow their own legal definitions and rules of procedure.

The crime of possessing anti-Soviet literature was the cornerstone of the entire Soviet system of oppression. In their way of doing things, there was no dispute about whether the crime was committed – after all the literature was in their possession and the judges defined what "anti-Soviet" meant. The only hope was to find a procedural violation.

There are many differences between common law and civil law (Continental European) systems of criminal trials. The one that intrigued me in the Soviet trials was the access of the trial judge to the dossier or file prepared by the *procuror* (prosecutor). The civil law judge may, indeed is required to read the entire file or dossier before the trial begins. The reason for this is that the judge directs the trial and he must know evidence in order to question the witnesses properly. This stands in sharp contrast to the common law practice, which insists that the judge and jury be totally ignorant of the evidence at the beginning of the trial.

The common law practice is thought to be strongly connected to the presumption of innocence. It is possible to imagine the common law defendant innocent – even though he or she has been indicted and brought before the court – because none of the evidence has been heard. In the Soviet and Continental systems, it has been more difficult to recognize the presumption of innocence because it seems like a direct threat to the competence of the procuracy, semi-judicial figures, who presumably would not have brought the defendant to trial if they had not diligently heard the evidence and concluded that the defendant was guilty.

In the early 1970s, I had published articles about the intensive debate in the Soviet literature whether the presumption of innocence could exist in the Soviet law. I even got into a dispute with Harold Berman, professor of Soviet Law at Harvard, about the issue because he, following the Whorfian hypothesis, argued that "presumption" was a Latin word and therefore not comprehensible to those who spoke Russian. I thought this application of the idea that language influences thought to be ridiculous – probably too strong an opinion for a young scholar hoping, perhaps, for the approval of his elders.

The great danger of the dossier system is that the judge will simply rubber-stamp the conclusions of the procuracy. For that reason, the RSFSR Code of Criminal Procedure introduced the critical principle that all the evidence of guilt must be heard in open court. The judge could not simply say, I see in the file that there are three witnesses who said that you robbed the store, therefore I find you guilty. In principle, the witness must be called and examined, just as in an American trial, though there might be more tolerance in the Continental trial for the use of a written statement in the dossier as a form of proof. But at least the document must be read aloud in court, with the defendant having a chance to question its accuracy.

In our cases of possessing anti-Soviet literature – so far as we could tell – the judge always had a statement in the dossier concluding that the literature was anti-Soviet. An agency of the KGB called *Glavlit* or *Oblit* prepared these statements. Once they were in the file, the judges were constrained not by the law but by the political nature of the system. They could not risk an open courtroom dispute about whether Zionist literature was really anti-Soviet or where Zionism was a politically acceptable ideology. Therefore the standard practice was for the judge to read the material in the dossier and proceed on the assumption that the KGB classification was correct. We concluded this on the basis of the testimony of the family members who had been in court and witnessed the proceedings.

The failure to read the *Glavlit* analysis in court, if true, was a clear violation of Article 301 of the RSFSR Code of Criminal Procedure, which says explicitly: "The court shall find the judgment solely on evidence which has been considered at the judicial session." The violation of this provision provided a politically safe way to convict the defendants of possessing illegal literature, and that charge in turn facilitated the charge of treason, which in the Soviet system meant no more than leaving the country illegally with the intent to compromise the interests of the Soviet Union. If the attempted Leningrad hijacking had a Zionist purpose, this was sufficient to characterize the action as attempted treason. This was the argument that led initially to the imposition of the death penalty. At the time, hijacking was not a specifically defined crime in the Soviet Union. It did not matter: the combination of possessing anti-Soviet literature and attempted treason gave the prosecution a more dangerous instrument of repression.

The lynchpin for their entire strategy was the practice of judges to convict without reading the dossier out loud in court and without permitting argument about the nature of Zionism and the possessed literature. Focusing on this procedural violation gave us a point of attack. We had a theory but no written papers to submit to the Soviet authorities. We had a lot of work ahead of us.

## *Cloak and Paper*

In April 1974, Telford and I took our first trip to the Soviet Union. The purpose was to seek a meeting with Rudenko to explain the project to him, and get his permission to submit our briefs. We arrived at one of the Intourist Hotels in Moscow, where only tourists with *valuta* (foreign convertible currency) were permitted to stay. I had been there before with academic groups, so I felt good returning to a familiar scene where I knew the language – at least better than 99% of the other tourists. I loved the life at these hotels in the center of Moscow. The breakfasts consisted of caviar, white fish, hard dark bread, and terrible coffee. You could buy a cup of cappuccino by waiting in a special line and paying *valuta*. I would pick up a copy of *Izvestia* or *Pravda* (the only newspapers then available) and read it over breakfast.

On that trip Telford and I spent a lot of time together over meals and waiting for the phone to ring. Most of the time we were trying to figure out how we could see important people in the legal establishment but we had many private moments in which he seemed to want to talk about his personal life and the decisions he had made. He was about to marry a young woman whose parents were younger than I. In those times, that surprised me but it would not today. In retrospect, I was the old man in the conversation, Telford was the innocent, the young one thinking about love and how to act on it. I listened patiently and appreciated the trust he showed in me.

In terms of our mission, our trip was a big gamble. We did not really have anything yet, just a plan and some convictions about the trials. I think Telford wanted some assurance that we would not spend time preparing the papers for nought.

I was used to the idea that if you went on a mission of this sort you would be followed and your room would inevitably be bugged. There were jokes about the suspicious tourists complaining about their dirty towels in the seeming privacy of their room and finding fresh new towels an hour later. This is possible but there were so many foreigners like us wandering around the Kremlin that it would have taken a small army of eavesdroppers to keep track of us all. Nonetheless, I had my favorite wannabe spy techniques. Of course in the plane coming over, I ripped up my notes and flushed them down the john. In Moscow itself there was a conventional method for evading followers. You boarded the metro – and savored the great artistic achievement of Moscow – got off at any station, crossed over and boarded the train going the opposite way. If you did this a few times, and you saw the same person changing trains with you, you had him. Of course, you could not do much about it, but at least you knew how important you were. Frankly, whenever I tried this switching technique, I never found anyone following me.

By Friday afternoon it seemed unlikely that anyone from the procuracy would call us in for a meeting. Taylor describes the mood in his fine narrative of the entire project, *Courts of Terror: Soviet Criminal Justice and Jewish Emigration* (Vintage 1976, 30-31):

"Fletcher and I had given up hope and were resigned to go home empty-handed. Fletcher had been eager to spend time in the bookshops. There seemed to be no reason for him to hang by the telephone any longer, and around four o'clock he left the hotel."

About an hour later the phone rang. The First Deputy of Rudenko, M.P. Malyarov, summoned Telford for a meeting. Telford speculates in his book that perhaps they knew about my absence. We will never know whether we were so closely watched and whether they would not have called, had I stayed with Taylor the whole time.

Telford explained the project to him – how we got our evidence on the basis of interviews of the relatives in Israel, how we had formulated preliminary judgments about possible illegalities in the trials. It is remarkable that Malyarov did not throw him out. But I can say from my subsequent interactions with the top Soviet officials, they never behaved discourteously. He agreed to receive the petitions from Telford. The first part of the mission was successful. The general and his sidekick Fletcher could mount their airborne steeds and return to the ranch with satisfaction that they had established contact with the "culprits" on the other side.

After classes were over in May 1974, Dershowitz assembled and directed an effective team of lawyers and students at Harvard.

We worked long hours together to produce four general legal memoranda on the issues and two dozen individual briefs on the particular defendants. It was an exciting time for me. I felt that for the first time in my life, I was part of a project of great meaning and that I could contribute with skills, such as my languages, which I had acquired for no particular reason but which turned out to be of great value.

In the end, the technical validity of the arguments depended on my interpretations of the Soviet legal materials, which were all available at the Harvard Library. The research fell on me. Lipson helped out a bit but I do not recall an incident in which he questioned my view of the Soviet legal materials.

Alas, as soon as the brief-writing project was completed in June, I had to return to LA with my family. Lipson and Taylor had the pleasure of taking the package of petitions to Rudenko's office. On this trip Rudenko did receive them and engaged in some discussion of the cases. Though he steadfastly denied that anything might be wrong with the prosecutions, he acknowledged that there was no statute covering hijacking at the time. That is why they had to use the treason statute and, in addition, the prohibition against stealing large quantities of state property. The latter charge did not expose the same procedural irregularity and was therefore more difficult for us to challenge.

The fact that they received Taylor and accepted the petitions represented a chip in the iron curtain separating the legal systems. It would be 15 years before the Berlin Wall would finally fall, but our intervening on the basis of Soviet law and their recognizing in fact what we were doing was a significant shift in the ideology that made the wall necessary.

Lipson and Taylor spent a week enjoying early summer in Moscow. They went home determined to wait for good news. By March 1975 nothing had happened, and I happened to be in New York to do research in the Columbia library and of course I went to look up Telford, whom I admired so much. He was then married to Toby Golick, the younger woman he mentioned in our earlier conversations. They lived right around the corner from Columbia and were about to start raising a family. In the course of our coffee, Telford dropped the question. "Are you free to go to Moscow right now?" In fact I was. It was spring break, no classes. My research could wait. I did not have my passport but my wife sent it to me the next day and soon I was off on a mission of my own. This was the first time that anybody in this project went alone to communicate with the top Soviet authorities. Taylor had some additional papers to submit and he wanted to know whether there was any point in waiting longer. Inevitably I acquired other duties such as checking with Ida Nudel on the status of the prisoners. She was the person in Moscow who kept closest track of the conditions in the labor camps.

I loved the adventure of going it alone, speaking Russian with everyone, taking time off to visit the theater when I could get tickets, as well as doing my job. Taylor mentions in his book that I was detained at the airport for 40 minutes and then perhaps in compensation "billeted in a most luxurious penthouse in the Intourist Hotel." What he does not mention is that this time, traveling alone, I assumed that my fantasy of finding a KGB-sent blonde waiting for me in my room would finally come true. No such luck. I hit the sack after a long trip and slept for ten hours.

I arrived on March 2 and by March 4, I had a tentative meeting set up with Tsibulnik at the procuracy. We had learned that he was the primary buffer between outsiders and higher officials in the procuracy. Here is my report written at the time, as published by Taylor on page 63:

"Promptly at 11:00 a.m. I am ushered into the office of Tsibulnik. We begin in Russian and get right down to business. He is stern, direct, and slightly nervous. He is smoking intensely. I explain my purpose of delivering the briefs and the letters. He berates me with rhetorical questions about the propriety of intervening in the Soviet legal system. I reply that I conceive of the work as a form of international legal cooperation. He questions me at length about the people involved in the project and the nature of Taylor's activities in the US. I explain what an American law firm is and the meaning of the letterhead on Taylor's stationary.

"A secretary is present. At some point, he begins to dictate to the secretary concerning the documents received. He becomes upset by thinking that the Grillius affidavit is not mentioned in the letter to Rudenko. I point out to him that in fact it is mentioned. They all address me as Georgij Nikolaevich – a comradely form of address in Russian – and seem to enjoy the pretense that I am one of them. At one point Tsibulnik asks me to step outside and 'go for a walk,' which I do. After waiting for about twenty minutes I am invited to return. Nothing seems to have changed. Perhaps Tsibulnik is a little more relaxed. The discussion turns to more pressing matters. Can we expect a reply? When? Would they want me to leave my telephone number in Moscow? Is there a personal message from Rudenko to Taylor? The response to these matters is that there is no desire to talk further with me ('If we need we can contact you through Intourist'). No reply to the briefs could be expected for 'a year or two.' They would communicate directly with Taylor in New York. No personal message to Taylor at this time. Of course, I should tell Taylor that the procuracy has respectfully received the briefs and the letters."

Then there was my assignment to visit Ida Nudel. I had her address but in order to find her I had to take the train (after the theater of course) out to the suburbs and then start walking through the deep snow. I finally reached the correct house number and found her apartment. Knocking on the door late at night, I was surprised that Ida answered. We sat down at her tiny kitchen table and engaged in a two-hour conversation about the situation of the prisoners. I was not terribly interested, to tell you the truth, I was more concerned about the legal issues at stake. In any event, I don't recall hearing any horrendous tales of torture or patent violations of international law. My attitude must have revealed itself for I soon heard from the refusenik community in Moscow that Ida assumed that because of my attitude and my

*George in the USSR, 1985.*

perfect Russian, I must have been sent by the KGB. I took this to be a great compliment.

My contacts on this trip were our final communication from Moscow concerning our legal arguments. Taylor decided at that point to go public and write his book laying out the details of our project.

Many of the people we took on as clients were eventually released and went to live in Israel. I would not say our legal intervention alone did the trick, but it was a factor, along with the political pressures and a general desire for East/West *détente* that led to the widespread exchange of prisoners.

In the years 1971-75, more than 113,000 Jews were allowed to emigrate from the Soviet Union, mostly to Israel. Ida Nudel immigrated to Israel with her sister and they lived together near Rehovot.

## *The Shcharansky Case*

As compared with our defendants, most of whom were rather simple people who wanted to live private lives, Anatoly Shcharansky was a public star from the very beginning of his intersection with the Soviet Jewry movement in the mid-1970s.

He became prominent just as Taylor was publishing his book. He started hanging out near the synagogue with the other Jewish dissidents and then rose quickly to a position of leadership. His efforts were highlighted by the founding of the Helsinki Watch Committee in 1975 and Jimmy Carter's election in 1976, which would lead to treating the emigration issue as a question of human rights. The foreign journalists sought out Anatoly because he commanded excellent English. The constant reporting of the refuseniks' plight put tremendous pressure on the Soviet regime.

The ground for Shcharansky's arrest on March 15, 1977 was alleged treason. The act that supposedly constituted his treason is not clear. We thought at the time that the primary allegation was that he made a secret drop-off of militarily sensitive information to Robert Toth of the Los Angeles Times. But why contacting foreign journalists should constitute treason is less comprehensible to me than the allegations of attempted treason based on leaving the country illegally with the intention of doing harm to the motherland.

We do know several critical features of his trial. The court allowed him to fire his lawyer and defend himself. This was a sure sign to us, as observers, that they would not impose the death penalty. They allowed him to make an opening statement of at least an hour. This kind of activism in court had been unheard of in a routine trial for possessing anti-Soviet literature. Also, they never had a defendant before who was a leading intellectual. The Soviet government, in my mind, was on a dangerous path. They might have thought that they were putting an end to the movement, but in many respects, this proved to be the last gasp of the entire governmental system of repression that began with the denial of the exit visas and the First Leningrad Trial in 1970.

This is not to downplay the cruelty and the legal arbitrariness of the verdict. Shcharansky received a 13-year sentence, of which he heroically served nine years in a *gulag*. Yet he was a much greater man than his adversaries. He maintained his sense of humor, managed to play chess with himself in his cell and keep a memorial record of everything he could write down in the best-selling book *Fear No Evil* as soon as he was released in a spy-trade in 1986.

I remember commenting about his release at the breakfast table. My younger daughter Rebecca, then 18 years old, had a spontaneous reaction: "Shcharansky? My God, I feel I have grown up with his case." In some respects she had. Lawyers all over the world had been working on the case from the day of his arrest in 1977.

Two things made his trial and imprisonment permanently newsworthy. First there was an entire group of dissident celebrities who showed up at his trial. Everyone from Yelena Bonner to Yuri Orlov was there. His mother kept a vigil at the court every day. Most importantly of all, his wife Avital, who had been permitted to leave for Israel before the arrest in 1977, became the indomitable lioness of the movement. She was everywhere – speaking, making new friends for the movement, meeting with lawyers who wanted to identify themselves with the cause. She was star material of the first order and the entire human rights world sought to be in her aura. Also, Irwin Cotler, later Minister of Justice of Canada, devoted himself to the case. He was the go-to person to find out the current state of play, as we had occupied that role for all the cases documented in Taylor's book.

The facet of the Shcharansky phenomenon that truly inspires is that the world kept his image alive while he was isolated, cut off from everyone, and trying to stay sane. He matured in his prison years so that when he was released and immigrated to Israel, he was ready for a significant political commitment. He simplified the spelling of his name (by dropping the difficult "shch" sound), changed Anatoly for the more Jewish Natan, and established a new political party to serve the growing number of Russian immigrants. He won elections, served as a minister in the government, became a best-selling author, and was even praised by President Reagan for his views on democracy. Whether

Anatoly or Natan, he has been a hero of the age. As chairman of the Jewish Agency, he continues to play an active leadership role in Israeli society.

Equally impressive is the complete turnabout of Avital. As soon as her husband flippantly zig-zagged in his walk across the line from East to West and, always keeping his sense of humor, apologized for being late, Avital turned inward. She put on a head scarf and sent her husband to synagogue (which he did not exactly like). Then she went into her "tent" to wait for the children that were overdue. I spent a Shabbat meal with them a few years ago. And having worked with Avital when she embodied the force of the movement I was impressed by her transition. It is moving to witness two human beings who had the character to do what they had to do when the times required it, but not allow their lives to be cast permanently by the needs of the moment.

## *Perestroika, Language and Law Reform*

By the time of Sharansky's release, Mikhail Sergeevich Gorbachev had become general secretary of the Communist Party. His programs – *perestroika* (restructuring) and *glasnost* (transparency) – were in full swing as the spy swap including Sharansky was negotiated. Other critical events of the late 1980s – the disaster at Chernobyl and the endless unsuccessful Russian intervention in Afghanistan – along with the failure of the government to manage the Soviet Jewry movement – led eventually to the dissolution of the link between the state and the Communist Party in 1990 and the conversion of the Soviet Union into a Commonwealth of Independent States in 1991.

I admired Gorbachev for his liberal tendencies and his gift with language. Soviet policy suddenly shifted from hard repression in criminal trials to a publicity campaign based on the invention of new labels. One of my favorites is the way Gorbachev invented the rule of law for his disappearing Soviet Union. The traditional Communist slogan since the time of Stalin was that the Soviets maintained "socialist legality." That meant that they would enforce the rules strictly, though we saw in our study of the anti-refusenik trials that not even this minimal demand was realized in practice. The alternative is the German idea of the *Rechtsstaat* – a state based on higher ideals of justice. It was difficult to express this idea in Russian, but Gorbachev correctly seized on the distinction between two different words for law – *zakon* and *prava* – to construct the idea. The former word means statute, acts of legislative will imposing rules from above. This was the foundation of "socialist legality." The alternative, based on the notion of *prava,* has built into it the ideas of justice and human rights. Gorbachev coined the term *pravovoe gosudarstvo* (government expressing the idea of rights) to capture this idea that aligns Soviet justice with the principles of the West.

In the early spring of 1989, I traveled to Gorbachev's USSR-in-transition with a Helsinki Watch mission to investigate changes in attitudes toward the rule of law. It became clear that Gorbachev was doing his best to resolve the most striking differences between Western and Soviet conceptions of the rule of law. He explicitly endorsed the presumption of innocence in a speech to the 19th Party Congress in 1988. He advocated the abolition of the crime of possessing anti-Soviet literature. There was even informal discussion of limiting the concept of treason to offenses comparable to the Smith Act in the US, namely advocating violent overthrow of the government. It is striking how much of the reform advocated by Gorbachev and his fellow liberals seemed to address the abuses that occurred in the prosecution of the Jewish refuseniks.

During my visit in those heady times I sat in to observe a trial in the Kiev central courthouse. It was a routine trial for embezzlement committed in the course of engaging in the shortcuts around the economic plan. But the stealing of state property was a theme the trial had in common with the First Leningrad trial. I was quite surprised at how open the lawyers and the defendants were. They were prepared to speak to me about everything. In the end, two defendants were convicted of embezzling state property in small quantities (below the threshold of the death penalty). The defendants and lawyers were skeptical about the possibility of an acquittal, but by and large, the trial seemed to be conducted according to the norms that would apply in any Western European courthouse.

But not everything in the new Soviet legal mind conforms to Western principles of justice. We encountered several Soviet scholars who supported a draft bill to reduce the scope of capital punishment by eliminating the economic crimes (like theft and embezzlement of state property in large quantities – the charges in the First Leningrad trial and in the one I observed in Kiev). That part of the reform was fine. More surprising was the planned exemption from the death penalty of men over 60 and women of any age. I found this genuinely puzzling. The rule of law is not only a system for conferring benefits on right-holders but also for ensuring equality in the distribution of burdens. One of my friends, an old-timer at the Institute of State and Law, Sofya Gregorovna Kelina, defended the proposed change with three arguments: (1) women never receive the death penalty anyway; (2) they have a special role in Soviet society; and (3) it is important to cut back capital punishment any way we can, and this way is politically acceptable.

The arguments are obviously specious as one could see immediately by substituting some ethnic group with a low crime rate – say Uzbeks – for women. It would strike everyone as absurd to use the example of an ethnic group, yet the provision for women passed legislative and even academic scrutiny without objection. You can't even call this affirmative action for women. It is simply an affirmative form of discrimination based on chivalry and the treatment of women as "special" beings. This "special" treatment of women seems to have disappeared in the code revision of 1996.

There are still people writing about Russian law, and some of them know Russian. But there are no longer distinguished scholars of the field, no chairs to be filled at the major law schools, no controversies in the literature – indeed no literature. The field has lost its glamour along with its military relevance. It was attractive when it was the enemy's law. It was interesting when it represented a different social system with different ideals. If it is just a shoddy version of Western European law, there is not much reason to study it.

A decade ago it was fashionable to send teams of lawyers to help the Russians and other peoples trying to craft democratic institutions to redraft their basic legal documents. I was skeptical about these efforts because the lawyers we sent did not speak Russian and did not understand the Russian system. It never works well for one system simply to transplant, say, its corporate law in another regime that is at a different stage of economic and cultural development. The desire for cooperation must come from the side that recognizes its need for advice.

Looking back on these trips and these intense writing projects, I feel fortunate to have been involved in a turning point of the cold war. I could express both my romantic love for Russian and the Soviet Union and my commitment to the Jewish people. For an academic lawyer, there is no greater thrill than stepping out of the office and actually engaging with the people who have your clients in their custody. For me this thrill is amplified enormously by the opportunity to represent my client in another one of my six foreign languages.

My life in Russian was surely as adventurous as my life in German. I found a political mission and savored the role of minor intermediary in the cold war. But I fear that the death of the Soviet Union has also brought about stasis in this side of my personality. I still speak Russian with a few people, but intensity of this life is on the wane. The past teaches me, however, that you never know when someone might look you up – as did Telford Taylor – and reinstate the need for a language that was once so valuable.

Chapter Four

# My Family: Hungarian

After the death of my uncle, Arnold Berk, in the 1970s, the family gathered the home of his widow Flora, not for a wake, but for a subdued conversation, perhaps about him, perhaps about aspects of the family.

An argument quickly erupted between my cousin Paul Geller and Flora's son-in law, Frank Lossy. The structure of the argument was very simple. It went something like this:

Frank: Our family is really Hungarian.

Paul: No it is not, it is Jewish. That is why he had a Jewish ceremony today.

Frank: Ceremonies don't mean anything. The culture, the ethnicity of our family is Hungarian.

Paul: Jewish

Frank: Hungarian

It went on like this for a few minutes until Paul, who is a genius in finding biting one-liners, finally said: "Oh, I get it. You are willing to trade five thousand years of grandeur for five hundred years of barbarism!"

Perhaps this riposte won the argument for the night, but it raises larger questions for me about the short term and long term identify of my family. Let me begin with my parents' stories as I remember them.

## *My Father's Story*

My father, born Fleischer Miklós (the Hungarian practice is to write the family name first) in 1897 in Szécsény, Hungary would have probably agreed with Frank. He was Hungarian, but in a very special sense that probably did not matter to Frank, namely the sense of the Hungarian nation that existed prior to the loss of 71% of its territory in the 1920 treaty of Trianon. The Hungarian nation, as it existed then, was an equal partner in the Austria-Hungarian Empire, with a cosmopolitan policy of inclusion. It held out the promise to the minorities of Eastern Europe that if they learned Hungarian, they would be Hungarian. The promise is similar to the one extended by the French in the last century. Whether they have always kept the promise is another story, but the idea was established – in both the cases of the French and the Hungarians – you learn our language, you become one of us.

When my father Miklós was growing up in Szécsény, he felt that he was a member of the Hungarian upper class. His father was a *főldbirtakos*, which meant that he was a large landowner, and this was enough to create a pretense at the time of being close to petty nobility. When the First World War began, he was inducted as an *ein jaehriger Freiwilliger*, which meant that he could qualify as an officer at the end of his training. I don't know how long or intensively he fought with his fellow Hungarians on the Eastern Front but soon he fell captive to the Russians and spent several years in a prison camp in the East. He was released in the summer of 1919 and trekked, over ground, without money, back to Hungary, only to discover that in the wake of the Kun Béla Communist revolution, the fascist counter-revolution released a vicious wave of anti-Semitism.

He went home to see his father, Fűlőp, who died in late 1919. The legend of the family is that he died out of fear that the Communists would take his land. On his death bed, his father advised him to leave and may have given him a jewel to tide him over. So far as I know, Miklós spent several months "down and out" in London and Paris – in the image of George Orwell. He made it to Spain but was expelled for leftist political activity. His two brothers Géza and Marci also left, both to the southern cone of Latin America, one to Argentina, the other to Chile. Amál, my father's sister, joined her brother in Santiago. It is not clear to me exactly in which years all this migration took place. Also, it is not clear what happened to my grandfather's estate, if it was not seized by the Communists and so far as I know, the six-month Communist regime did not have the time to carry out their land reform policies. A small grave in the Jewish cemetery in Szécsény marks my grandfather's memory as a great landowner in that small corner of Hungarian agriculture.

I should add a note about these names used in the family. Géza and Miklós are common Hungarian names. But Fűlőp, Marci, and Amál are rare. I cannot quite explain the penchant of my father's family for these unusual names. We shall see that the problem of naming on my mother's side had its own unique characteristics.

My father found his way to the United States, but not by normal means. He could not get a visa because the quota for Hungary was much lower than for, say, Poland or Russia. He went to Mexico, spent some time there, and then hired a "coyote" to lead to him to the Rio Grande. Of course my father insisted that the "coyote" go first for the sake of security. Eventually my father was left on his own – he swam across the river to North America. He landed near El Paso and from there he hopped a freight train going north to Saint Louis. This was a critical moment. Would he try to blend into American society or stick to the small groups of Hungarians he could find? In the beginning of his adventures in the states he had little choice: he bonded with the Hungarians he could find. When he got to Saint Louis, he found lodging in the home of a Hungarian rabbi and stayed there until the rabbi discovered him smoking on Shabbat in the bathroom. Actually the neighbor saw the smoke and reported him. (Smoking – and all fires – are prohibited on Shabbat.)

For Miklós, the binding rules were not Jewish but the

cultural norms of his Hungarian class. He felt dishonored that he had gotten caught for cheating on the rabbi and therefore he felt compelled to leave. He went to nearby Chicago, which was booming at the time, and there he started to work at blue collar jobs, but as the son of a rich landowner, he had no skills. He tried to learn construction skills by showing up on the job and imitating the others, but he would always get fired within the first few hours. Eventually he picked up enough by watching others to become a house painter, a skill that he practiced for some 15 years.

He met my mother, Fanny, in a *kultúrklub*, a social club for Hungarians – effectively for Hungarian Jews whether they were religious or not. These were the kinds of people that hung out in my living room for my entire youth.

Miklós laid down the law that our home would not be Jewish, yet my mother, like a Spanish converso guarding her ancestral memory, lit candles most Friday nights, and my father brought her flowers every Friday night, a custom that I maintain to this day with my wife. So far, it looks like Frank's vision of the family as Hungarian rather than Jewish was proving to be correct. But Frank's wife, my cousin Rella Berk Lossy, was a knowledgeable Jew in hiding, much more learned than my mother or any of her sisters. When my father died in 1960, she taught me how to say the Kaddish, the prayer for the dead. The Jewish strain remained, even if it went underground.

Unfortunately, there was no master program for maintaining the Hungarian language in the US. If there were classes, they were probably taught by the Hungarian Catholic Church, as Greek is taught by the Greek Church. Nonetheless, my sister Lillian Peggy Rella, Lillian for short, nine years older than I, learned Hungarian as her first language. After her disappointing experience trying to play with children who spoke other languages, my parents decided to switch to English in speaking with their children. My sister quickly forgot her Hungarian, and when I came around, my parents still spoke Hungarian among themselves, but a rather weak English with me.

This was a tragic mistake. Lillian would eventually have learned English on the streets, and better English than my parents could have taught her. And by speaking English to me, my parents deprived me of a valuable gift, not only of a native speaker's knowledge of Hungarian, but the intimacy that would flow from my speaking their language. My mother could have addressed me in the same affectionate, idiomatic terms and told the same stories that her mother told her.

As I see it from the child's point of view, the parents' making a decision of this sort is an act of an injustice against the powerless child. The child hears the language of intimacy between the parents but cannot enter their circle and there is no way, on his own, as a child, that he can learn the language.

Two parents – even one parent – speaking to a child and correcting the child's feedback is enough to impart a language. It is an amazing phenomenon. And it takes virtually no intelligence and no work. The less educated classes, without thinking about it, do it all the time.

There were moments when I felt enormous shame not being able to speak Hungarian. It was equivalent to not being able to read one's native language. Many friends of my parents would ask and I would respond *egy kicsit* – "a little." The critical moment occurred when I was seven and living in Glendale. My grandmother had left Budapest and was on her way to live with her children in Latin America (I am not sure which one). I encountered her alone in the backyard and she tried to communicate with me. I could not say anything in response. My memory of the incident is one of powerlessness and shame.

Of course, I don't know whether my enormous interest in languages would have emerged spontaneously if I had not experienced this form of powerlessness as a child. There is no doubt that I think of language as a corrective for being dumb and silent in the face of an important person seeking to communicate with me. As a practical matter, if you are the one in the room who speaks the relevant language, you have a tremendous advantage over your contemporaries. I have discovered this over and over again in legal matters. In matters of the heart, as well, a language can make the difference between a successful marriage and a mutual groping in the dark. As we shall see in the next chapter, my entire life changed because later in life I was able to address an attractive woman in Spanish. This was partial redemption for that moment of embarrassment in my backyard in Glendale. The advantages of languages have repeatedly proven themselves to me. In the world of the monolingual, the person with an able tongue is – well, not king, but definitely, much to be admired.

## *My Mother's Story*

My mother, Fanny, was the third of seven siblings who lived together in two rooms at the center of a little town called Nagymihaly in northern Hungary. The town was situated in one of the places in Eastern Europe that was constantly undergoing a change of national identity. At the time it was part of Hungary and thus part of the Austro-Hungarian empire, which included lands stretching as far East as Cracow, now in Poland. My grandfather, Henrik, started his journey in Tarnov, a city near Cracow, and made his way West within the empire to settle in Nagymihaly. He was always a Polish citizen, which, as we shall see, had its advantages. His surname was Rand, meaning "the edge" in German, not a typically Jewish name. When he courted and then married Bella Blau in Nagymihaly, her name became Randova (the feminine form of Rand) in her Polish papers.

Coincidentally, Henrik's sister married Bella's brother, thus my mother has a set of cousins by the name of Blau. Two of these cousins are worth mentioning because their children still have an impact on my life. They are Esther and Manou. I picked up their story in the section devoted to my Israeli family.

The first-born child of Bella and Henrik, Rella (the first) was apparently very talented and ambitious. When she was in her teens, she started secretarial school in Kassa, now called Košice in Slovak. It was about an hour a way by public transportation. The others stayed and took whatever schooling was offered to them locally. My impression is that they did not stay in school past the age of 14. Harry, the oldest boy, received a good Jewish education in the synagogue on the main street. He learned to lead services as the representative of the community and surprised many of us, years later, when he got up at my daughter Rebecca's bat mitzva, and fluently "davened Musaf" – that is, he stood at the lectern with his back to the congregation and led us all in chanting the second service of the day. This seems like a great achievement to me but I think it was normal for any Jewish boy who grew up before World War II in that part of the world.

The family was poor. My grandfather was a tailor in the same small town. He was a lean, meek man. But our grandmother seems to have been just the opposite. The image of our brave and dauntless grandmother Bella was captured in a family picture. A heavyset woman, seen stirring a huge pot in the courtyard of our modest quarters, she is surrounded by many of the children.

Life was well-ordered in Nagymihaly, with symbols of both heaven and hell nearby. One symbol of both was the synagogue across the street. Our conception of heaven was the *cukrazda*, the pastry shop, a half block down the street. If Harry could scrape together a few pennies to buy a *krémes* – something like a napoleon – he was in bliss. He was always a sensual man, for good or for ill, and his career might have begun with addiction to pastry.

This addiction is quite common to Hungarians. The finest institutions in the society are the coffee houses and the little restaurants that serve *palacsinta*. Gerbeaux in Budapest is probably the most elegant café and pastry shop in the world. I too find it hard to resist these fine pastries, which, alas, are rarely to be found outside of Hungary. Israel is or at least was a good location for cafes because the Hungarian Jews took their crafts with them to Israel, their finest being pastry and humor (Ephraim Kishon being the greatest comedian import). New York, which used to have good Eastern European bakeries and a first rate

Hungarian restaurant, has become a desolate zone in which the traditional smells and tastes have lost out to chain stores making muffins and doughnuts.

The coherent little world of nine, seven children and two parents, blew apart in the aftermath of the First World War. In the war itself, as my mother relates the story, they had to flee the city and hide in the forest, but that was not the worst of it. After the Treaty of Trianon in 1920, Nagymihaly became part of Slovakia, in turn part of Czechoslovakia. The official language of the region shifted from Hungarian to Slovak, a language my family could not speak at all. They suddenly became even more marginal than they had been as Jews.

Romance proved to be the way out. Rella, the independent one who studied in the next town, had a beau, Arnold Berkowitz (later shortened to Berk), from the next village. They would sneak out together to the local movies and pay my mother hush money to cover for them. When they decided to marry, they found objections on all sides. There was nothing wrong with Arnold. But there was a difference of class that no one today would notice. Arnold's family were small shopkeepers. My grandfather was a lowly tailor. A marriage between these two classes offended the order of the day.

This was a blessing in disguise. Arnold had some relatives in Chicago. Arnold and Rella decided to elope and make their way in the US. This is the point at which the Polish nationality of my grandfather came in handy. The immigration quota from Poland was higher than those either from Czechoslovakia or Hungary. Rella could immigrate as a Pole. I am not too sure how Arnold did it.

Rella quickly realized that the economic opportunities in Chicago were much greater than in Nagymihaly. She found a job in a bank, which made the family enormously proud of her. To her great merit, she went back to her native village and convinced the other eight members of the family to emigrate. They started leaving, sometimes two together, sometimes one alone, all with

Polish passports.

At the age of 16, in 1922, my mother made the trip by herself. She knew no language other than Hungarian. That she managed this voyage by herself amazes me. My hunch is that she had a good time on the ship. Margaret and Flora made the trip together and Margaret, still flourishing today at 98, loves to recount her adventures as a young woman crossing the ocean.

Before they all made it to Chicago, disaster struck. Rella, the great heroine of the saga, gave birth to a little boy named Richard, known in the family as Dickie. Then she was stricken with a fatal disease, to the best of my knowledge leukemia. She died quickly, a tragic but Romantic end to an iconic figure who saved an entire family from the Holocaust.

Arnold was stuck with the responsibility of earning a living, supporting the other members of the family just getting off the boat, and taking care of an infant. My grandmother Bella intervened and according to one version of the story, invented something like a female version of leverite marriage in Deuteronomy 25. The Biblical principle is that if a woman marries and her husband dies leaving her childless, it is the duty of next son in line to marry the woman, give her a child, and perpetuate the family name. There are elegant rituals for getting around this duty, also mentioned in Deuteronomy 25, and I don't think that the rule is ever enforced except among communities that, shall we say, are a little isolated and backward. According to Grandmother Bella Rand's adaptation, however, the daughter next in line was required to marry Arnold in order to take care of the child. You can see the obvious differences with leverite marriage, but I guess the Rand sisters were not very good lawyers or they could not stand up to their mother's dictates. The duty fell upon Flora. I am not sure why. My mother was older but perhaps she was already engaged or married to my father. In any event, Flora was required to marry Arnold.

I had a lot of affection for both Arnold and Flora. Arnold was the only member of the family who was more interested in weight lifting than discussing politics. He ran a gym in Chicago and later in Southern California, he became a chiropractor and opened up a Health Food Store in El Monte, on the east side of Los Angeles. When I was in high school and could drive, I sometimes went to work there as a waiter behind the counter. Arnold used to give me health tips. He used to say, "If you take a cold shower every morning you will never get a cold." The truth is that it worked (at least I never got colds).

One night when I was about 20 years old and on break from my studies at Cornell, I came home late after seeing "A Room at the Top," a powerful story of lust and adultery with Laurence Harvey and Simone Signoret. The family was there playing cards and chess and testing which aunt made the best pastry. (Of course, not to be outdone, they lied to each other about their recipes.) The room was brimming with laughter but Flora noticed my disorientation and asked what was bothering me. I told her that I was confused by the sympathetic portrayal of adultery in the film. She took me aside, smiled, and said, "Georgie, you have to understand, sometimes a woman has to do what she has to do." That was my way of learning not to judge the sexual practices of the women in my family.

Flora had the sharpest tongue I have ever encountered. If you brought her the wrong gift, she would snap, "Take that to the people down the street." Yet she was very compassionate and always communicated her love for me – at least while Arnold was still alive. Later, after she remarried a lovely man – also a Hungarian Jew – named Gene, I had the temerity to ask her in front of Gene about the obligatory marriage to Arnold. She did not speak to me for several years.

She and Arnold had a daughter, whom they named Rella. She was the Rella Berk who eventually married Frank Lossy. That she carried the name of Arnold's deceased wife always seemed to me an insult to Flora, but we have to remember the extraordinary reverence the family tendered for the original Rella.

Rella Berk became an important figure in my life. She had a

strong artistic streak and passed some of it down to my daughter Rebecca. I always wondered how the Rands converted themselves from a family of peasants to a collection of artists and intellectuals. The tactics of marriage played a critical role.

### *The Artistic Turn*

The first marriage of importance was with my younger Uncle Alex, sixth in the birth order of the Rand family. He was an extraordinarily handsome man. With sleek black hair and an engaging smile, he looked like Rudolph Valentino. He was not well-educated, but eager to learn. He was never exposed to music in Nagymihaly, but then as he told me the story, he entered a church one day when the organ was playing. The music transported him. His life changed. From then on, women and song were far more important than wine, money or other possible competitors.

Because of his charm and stunning good looks, he could attract a wife who came from a class of wealthy, well-educated Berliners. Lola was a woman of much learning and many talents. She was total female. You could never see her in the morning before her two hour toilette, during which she prepared to meet the public. She had a wonderful operatic voice and became a raconteur of jokes and stories in Yiddish and several other languages. Though she did not speak Hungarian, she could keep the family in stitches for hours. She became the language coach for the Chicago Opera and her and Alex's home became a salon for music lovers. Her marrying Alex had a deep impact on the values of our uneducated immigrant clan.

Lola became an artistic role model for Rella Berk in Chicago. When she was of college age, however, Rella Berk left and studied creative writing at the University of Iowa. She also mastered the piano and there seemed to be no limits to her talents. She found her way out to Berkeley, which was the appropriate move for intellectuals in those days. She was living there in the International House, when my mother informed Frank Lossy, a friend of the family and then a young dashing psychoanalyst, of a family member who had moved into the neighborhood. Frank made a date with a Rella to meet her at her rented piano studio. Of course, Rella made him wait until she was done with her practice session.

It took a few years of courtship for them to marry, greatly enhancing our family by bringing Frank into it. Exogamy has served us well, because of the few like Alex and Rella Berk had strong instincts to bring into the family what we needed – artists and intellectuals. At the age of 16, I was old enough to make the trip from Los Angeles to Carmel to attend the vows of marriage written by Frank and Rella. I and everybody else in the family was shocked that Frank and Rella chose to get married in a social hall with a judge. Forget the rabbi and the proscribed ritual. They wrote the whole ceremony themselves. How was that possible? I was amazed by my newly discovered sense of how individuals could direct their own lives.

From that day on I walked in their shadow. I may have argued with them to test my wits but I imitated nearly everything they did – well, not everything. I found my own way on a couple of matters. I thought it was snobbish of them to drive identical VW bugs when that was the car of Berkeley intellectuals. I would not buy a German car when that form of abstinence seemed to make a statement (I did not have any money so making this statement was easy). Frank spoke good Spanish and I recall meeting him in Spain, with Rella, in the summer of 1964. At the moment I could barely get out a few words in Spanish. The next year, Frank swears, I encountered him again, speaking fluent Spanish.

I copied Frank and Rella in other matters as well. If Frank hand-made his living room couch, I carpentered my desk. If they cultivated a taste for Latin American arts, I did the same. The only matter on which I maintained a distinctive path was my approach toward Judaism. I recognized in Frank my father's intellectual brand of atheism – and my decision had implicitly been to stay close to my father by refusing to assimilate into American culture.

Thus it seemed that I should have followed Frank on this matter, but I did not. For the generation of my father and Frank's father, religion was anathema. That included any form of being Jewish. Frank made an effort to stay Hungarian, at least in style. He named his first daughter Panna, which is supposed to be an ancient Hungarian name. There were always little touches of Hungarian culture in their house as in mine.

But for me, my best option in my time and place was to become Jewish rather than to accentuate my fading Hungarian ties. There must have been more to it than the psycho-dynamics of accepting or rejecting my father. I recall a moment in synagogue when my mother displayed great emotion. I could not quite believe it because she always seemed so controlled with me. That moment of released emotion communicated to me something positive about Judaism. The synagogue seemed like a place where repression ended and the unpredictable could begin. I still feel that way though I have little experience to support the sentiment.

For the cousins in my generation of the Rands, there was little drama about becoming either Jewish or Hungarian. Paul was interested in Judaism in his late teens but that disappeared quickly and no one learned Hungarian, even at the basic level at which I eventually taught myself to speak. The Jewish-Hungarian past became a shadow of our parents' lives – the folklore of quaint villages locked in a struggle between the coffee shop and the rabbi's table. Our history was always there, always rehearsed at family occasions, but it was becoming less and less an active force as the family was gradually being absorbed into American culture.

There were sparks of resistance. One interesting example was Béla, Paul's father, who was at ease both with being Hungarian and Jewish. On the streets of Haudúszoboszló, down the road from Debrecen, he acquired the personality of a salesman, someone who could talk to anyone, induce them to come into his shop, and make a sale. He saw Judaism more as an opportunity than as a threat. With his charm and openness, it is not a surprise that later in life when he was called Bill and living among Southern Californians, he was elected president of his Temple.

My father loved the Hungarian language because he associated it with his service to the Emperor Franz Josef. Perhaps because of age or circumstances, he was the only man I knew in our inner circle who had served in uniform in the Great War. He also communicated to me the burden and honor of imperialistic thinking.

Languages – plus a vague distaste for money – were our closest point of shared value. He was very happy that I learned German in high school, thrilled that I learned Russian in college and, I believe, happy in his heart that I grew up adverse to thinking like a capitalist.

## *Compensatory Moves*

I tried many ways to learn Hungarian on my own. When I was about 11 years old, my father and I made an effort to design our own curriculum. He agreed to teach five words a day. He picked various objects in his field of vision and told me their names in Hungarian. I still remember some of those first words: *ajto* for door, *virag* for flower. But this was not a promising track and it soon folded in on itself.

I searched for books and manuals, but there were not many around. Many books for tourists are structured for crisis situations. Therefore you get a long list of words you can try to say or point to if you are sick and need to communicate with a doctor. The same kinds of lists inform others with necessary communications for the tourist – like ordering in a restaurant or fixing a car. A good book on a language – I learned from studying Russian – focuses not on words but on sentences and phrases that are necessary for survival if you are parachuted into a remote part of the country with a day's rations. I made gradual progress with my hit and miss approach until the 1980s. I was getting good enough to hold a conversation with my mother and my relatives, even though they thought it was a little cute and would say things like, "Now he is practicing his Hungarian." I regret that my father never heard me speak his language. He died during my senior year of college, very content to know that I spoke German and Russian and would make my way in the world.

In the mid-1980s, I found myself at Columbia University with lots of Hungarians around – even a Hungarian coffee shop at the corner of Amsterdam and 111th Street. The amazing thing is that the Hungarian bakery is authentic. I cannot fathom how they are able still to make genuine Hungarian pastries. My Uncle Alex would think that he had found the original *cukrazda* on the main street in Nagymihaly.

The Hungarian influence is all around the Columbia neighborhood. At the corner of 113th Street and Riverside, there is a statue of Kossuth Lajos, the great hero of 1848 who came to the states and impressed American audiences with his speeches. The statue is an exact replica of one that I discovered while cycling through Northern Hungary in the town of Satoralja-ujhely. Apparently, Kossuth was a hero to the Jewish community in the portion of the town called Ujhely.

I bought an apartment right next to the statue. That was as good a reason as any, I thought, for sinking down roots in a part of Manhattan. For many years, one of our neighbors, Istvan Deak, the Columbia Professor of Hungarian History, used to come out and clean the statue. For that reason, during the years of haphazard graffiti in New York, the Kossuth statue always remained clean. It serves as a secular shine for the Hungarians who live within driving distance. Every March 15, the anniversary of the Revolution of 1848, they come from all corners and gather in front of the statue to honor the most famous Hungarian in New York – at least among the figures who have been memorialized in bronze on Riverside Drive.

At Columbia I found a good tutor, an exotic woman named Zsuzsa who came over to my apartment to converse with me in Hungarian and teach me idiomatic expressions. Like many beautiful Hungarian women, she was partly Gypsy. To my relief, she was married and not flirtatious. There was another Zsuzsa as well who was an exchange student from Hungary and needed a place to stay. I had ten rooms on the fifth floor next to the Kossuth statue so I thought it fair that she take one of them. My friend Jaime from Buenos Aires lived there for a while and fell in love with her. It turned out that her father was the head of the Ministry of Science in Budapest and treated me very well when I came for a visit.

During the late 1980s I commuted often to Los Angeles because my mother was ailing and apparently did not have long to live. These were the same years that Deborah, my daughter, gave birth to Rachel and had no place to live with her. They all moved in with my mother and her nurse and caretaker, a generous and strong woman named Evelyn Williams from Georgia who held the entire operation together with grace and dignity.

When my mother died in the spring of 1989, I decided that it was time for me to take off for an extended adventure in Hungary. Passing through on another trip, I had visited my colleagues in law at Eötvös Loránd University and told them I wanted to come as a visiting professor in the fall of 1990. They were thrilled. I would become the first visiting professor from the West. That I could speak to them in Russian put them at ease and the little Hungarian at my command was a plus. I knew that they probably did not have any money, but from my experience with Communist-run universities, I suspected that they had pots of dough for extras – like taking dignitaries to dinner, providing them hotel rooms, fine apartments, and cars. I told them I would work for free if they could come up with a nice apartment. The one they found on the left bank of the Danube was exquisite beyond my dreams. It had one large room facing the river and several smaller rooms in the back, a dark bedroom good for sleeping, a large, easily-flooded bathroom with a drain in the center and a convenience kitchen. The best part was the large balcony for sitting and observing the robust life below – ships moving up and down the Danube, the two old bridges, the Freedom Bridge to the left and the Chain Bridge to the right, and all the pedestrians walking across between the halves of Buda and Pest. The city is very proud of its bridges; my father's favorite was the Chain Bridge. In addition to being majestic works of art, these bridges are essential in keeping the two communities linked.

To the left of the Freedom Bridge stood the Gellért Hotel, the most famous hotel in town, known for it luxurious hot baths, and two swimming pools, one inside with hot baths and natural springs, the other, also fed by the same water but with artificial waves generated by a pump underwater. It was the place to go and spend a day lounging and imbibing in the coffee houses overflowing with delicious pastry or in one of the *söröző* – the beer bars that seem to be everywhere in the hotel. I heard my family say many times: "They went to Budapest and of course they stayed in the Gellért."

## *My 1989 Journey*

I would take up residence on the bank of the Danube in September when classes began. My first project was to take a long bicycle ride, a sentimental journey, to honor my mother. My destination was Nagymihaly, as the town was called in Hungarian. Now as part of Slovakia, it is called Micholovska, the meaning of "Michael the Great" retained. As I was riding north from Budapest I suddenly saw a sign pointing to Szécsény to the East. I had remembered my mother telling my about my father's birthplace and therefore I turned off the main road and found the village. I asked around whether there was a Jewish cemetery and found the last Jew alive in the town. His wife made it her job to look after the cemetery. She took me to the secluded place and within five minutes I found my grandfather's tombstone flush at ground level informing me in Hungarian that he died in 1919. The lettering was all in Hungarian, not Hebrew. This already said a great deal about the extent of his family's assimilation into Hungarian culture. Most of the other gravestones were written in the traditional style in Hebrew.

It was also significant that his forename Fűlőp was hardly a Hungarian name. The family name Fleischer is more German than Jewish and his first name (like mine) seems to me not Hungarian at all, but an expression of Anglophilia. I now bear his forename as my middle name Philip, but I have never heard of another Hungarian by that name. So it is apparent that we have an assimilated man buried in a Jewish cemetery. I think probably there was no choice. He could not have been buried in a Christian cemetery without converting, and presumably he did not want to do that. Many ambitious Hungarians did convert (recall the film *Sonnenschein*) but he obviously felt that being Hungarian at that period of time was a sufficient identity.

The positive side of Judaism – the part Paul described as 5,000 years of grandeur – differs from the negative side, which was all too common in Europe in the 19th century. The latter includes a list of horrors – anti-Semitism, shame, persecution, and an orthodox version of the religion full of primitive superstitions like breaking the necks of chickens by swinging them over your head to cast away your sins. My family – like most immigrant families from Eastern Europe – are experts in negative Judaism. None who lived in the United States retained the unthinking commitment to orthodoxy they learned as children. For my Uncle Harry – the man who loved the *cukrazda* – the decisive temptation was an ice cream cone during Passover (not allowed because of its bread-like base).

The family did not care much about the positive side either. For them, the Star of David represented the cruelty and prejudice of others, not the legacy of King David, the Book of Samuel, and the prophets.

There are two ways – perhaps three – to escape negative Judaism. One is immigrate to Israel, which, as I will relate later, a large part of my extended family has done and the other is to live in the West, as does Frank, believing that one's Eastern Europe connections are really about Polish, Russian, or Hungarian nationality and not about being Jewish. The third possibility, a rare option for those with dedication, is to study many years, to become learned about the grandeur of Judaism, and perhaps to become more respectful of the religious life as well. None of these extremes is easy, and therefore I blame no one who opts for the middle way of assimilation in the West.

My greatest attachment to Hungarian culture (the patriots will forgive me) is a dish that mother made. It is said that for the first five years of my life I ate nothing but *palacsinta*, a crepe-like dish with a filling of either nuts and sugar, apricot jam, or perhaps a special cheese found only in Hungary called túró. A correctly made *palacsinta* is very difficult to find in the world today. The best place is rural Hungary. Even in Budapest the restaurants make the dish too rich and fancy by dousing it in chocolate. They are a little ashamed of this simple peasant's dish. I guess in culinary circles, it is something like a hot dog, and you could not expect an expensive restaurant in New York to serve a good hot dog.

After visiting my grandfather's grave in 1989, I found a restaurant around the corner that served first-rate *palacsinta*. Curiously, when I went back to the same site last summer I had trouble finding the grave, perhaps because the grass was overgrown. After giving up, I thought my consolation would be the *palacsinta* next door. That place did not serve food anymore but next to it, in the garden, I found a high quality *palacsinta* that could not be matched in any big city of the world. Interestingly though, the shape was slightly different. Typically, *palacsinta* is made in a round roll like a crepe. This one was flat with the edges folded over. My cousin Karen and I discussed the relative merits of this shape for at least an hour.

Excuse me for spending more time on the shape of *palacsinta* than on Hungarian grammar. It is a matter of priorities.

But we must give grammar its due. The basic structural features of the language are not so difficult, but of course different from every other language. The simple part is that there is no gender difference even in the pronouns. I always thought this was a feature engineered by Hungarian men (or women) so that they could talk about their lovers without a third person in the room knowing whether the person spoken about was male or female. "Yes, dear, I am having coffee with (him/her) later today." The listener does not know the gender of the person being met for coffee. Some languages are obsessed with gender, even to the point of distinguishing between male and female in the second person (for example, Hebrew and Arabic). Hungarian is the ideal language for adulterers and feminists. The former can conceal their dalliances more easily and the feminists never have to fight about whether to say he or she.

The peculiarity of Hungarian is its obsession with spatial relationships. It is almost as though Hungarians speak in the dark and through their language create a world that the eye cannot see. They distinguish between the conjugation of verbs when there is a defined and undefined direct object. If one says "I love you," that is one form, but if one says "I love everything" the verb form is different. Then for some reason the third person as the object of the verb is considered different from the first and second persons. The third person takes the conjugation of defined objects. All of this is mysterious, but I am convinced that built into it is a philosophical view of the world that I have not yet decoded. This world view is characteristic of all Turkish languages (and Hungarian is one of them).

The obsession with spatial relations continues with an array of suffixes that informs the listeners exactly how one object makes contact with another. Does one object go on top of the second, under it, beside it, up to it, beyond it? Or just how does it make contact? One must know these in order to engage in the simplest tasks of life, such as playing marbles. Again, I am convinced that Hungarians see spatial relations more acutely than speakers of other languages. Of course what they see is not limited by their language. Presumably they see the difference between men and women, even though their pronouns are neutral on this point.

We have decided to remain agnostic in this book about

the Whorfian hypothesis that language influences modes of thought. If I allowed myself to indulge in the Whorfian way of thinking, however, I would say that Hungarian grammar explains why Hungarians have a propensity to excel at chess and why a Hungarian architect named Ernő Rubik invented Rubik's Cube, the three-dimension brain-twister that requires the problem-solver to think on several planes at once.

My nostalgic trip to Nagymihaly continued without great adventure. I crossed the border to Slovakia and then rode across the mountains from Košice to Nagymihaly. I had a sense that I already knew that route because of the family stories of my oldest aunt, Rella, taking the streetcar to Košice to attend secretarial school. There is no streetcar anymore and cycling the relatively deserted stretch, it is hard to believe that there ever was one. Yet the story of Rella's making that trip was important. For a family of peasants where someone might aspire to be a tailor, this was a high achievement. It meant that she could actually get a white collar job in a bank or an office. With the job she eventually got in a bank in Chicago, she was able to lead the family migration to the United States.

Eventually I rolled into Nagymihaly and found comfortable accommodations for my bicycle and myself in the penthouse of the new Communist-style skyscraper hotel at the end of the main street. The whole town was not very large and I could easily stroll from the hotel to the center where, according to the family stories, there once stood a synagogue and our family residence across the street. The synagogue had been converted into the Communist Party headquarters, and the family residence – two rooms and a courtyard they called home – had been torn down and a department store built in its place. There was also a good Hungarian library half way down the block and still standing was the *cukrazda* that filled the fantasy life of my Uncle Harry. The leading item in the shop – in Harry's time and in 1989 – was the *krémes* – the napoleon or *mille feuille* with creme-filled crusts.

There was not much to do there. No family to look up.

No interesting sights to see. I did not know where the Jewish cemetery was, but I had no desire to see it. Nagymihaly defines the homeland but no one from my mother's family is buried there. The library was interesting for about half an hour. It was enough for me just to be in that place of memory. And, of course, one of the advantages of cycling as a mode of travel is that just plain rest is much appreciated.

I tried to link the various places I saw with the seven brothers and sisters. In order of their birth, they were Rella, Harry, Fanny (my mother), Flora, Margaret, Alex, and Elizabeth. I could imagine the entire brood in the town square of Nagymihaly, though they rarely existed for me as a collective. In my mind they came in pairs or as individualists. Rella stood by herself as the heroine of the family. My mother and Harry (often called poor Harry because he always seemed to fail at business) were bound by a deep affection. My mother looked after Harry financially, and Harry felt a love for my mother that exceeded even my own. At her funeral, in 1989, of course I cried and recited the Kaddish. It was one of the saddest moments of my life, but I felt an urge to live and flourish on my own. Harry, by contrast, made a serious effort to throw himself into the grave with Fanny.

Flora and Margaret were bound together because they made the trip across the ocean together. But I never sensed much affection between them. Alex and Elizabeth were special as the two youngest. After Elizabeth divorced her American husband, Bill, the first American-born person to marry into the family, Alex tried to convince Elizabeth that she should lead a life of sexual emancipation. I think this gave him vicarious pleasure. But I could not believe that anyone in this family required this lecture.

The spouses of these seven had very little in common. Arnold Berk was the he-man, a man of courage and commitment who took the lead to leave the old country. There was nothing too difficult for him. Perhaps he was not the most intellectual uncle but he had an admirable character. To get his chiropractor's license in California, he got up every morning at dawn to study before going to work. The others were businessmen of varying degrees of success. My father was too gentle a man, too interested in others, to take profit-making seriously. Harry's wife, Matti, was probably the most charming of all the aunts but she could not do much besides work in a department store. Béla, Margaret's husband, was the stunning financial success and, for me, the most intriguing character in the family. He cut a dramatic figure, a swashbuckler reeking with stories and adventures. Alex's wife, Lola, was the artistic inspiration and the most learned. She was the only one who knew Hebrew and had an exquisite collection of Jewish silver artifacts, which because of my Jewish interests, she generously bequeathed to me (along with all of her German books, which were much more than I could handle). The young American Bill Elden, married to Elizabeth, the only native speaker of English, was an accountant and therefore trusted. He was often called in to mediate family business disputes.

On the ride back in 1989 there was only one amusing incident. I crossed an unguarded border on a small road between Slovakia and Hungary and kept riding as though everything was normal. About a hundred yards into Hungary, a police officer jumped out from behind the trees and demanded to see my papers. I thought this was very funny but then I recalled the historical situation. This was the time of transition in Eastern Europe from state socialism to democratic capitalism. Many people were escaping from the Eastern countries to Hungary as the moral liberal portal to the West. I had just crossed a sensitive boundary. And the poor officer, stationed behind his tree, had nothing to do unless a hiker or cyclist or suspicious car passed by.

## *Living on the Bank of the Danube*

My apartment on the Danube fulfilled all my fantasies of Hungarian daily life. There was a block-long stall market at the corner near the entrance to the Freedom Bridge. I went there every morning to buy a piece of good pastry, a newspaper, usually the *Uj Nemzet* (the New Nation) because I liked the style of print, and perhaps some green or red peppers, the basic stock of the Hungarian diet. I brought these and enjoyed my feast on an antique desk near the front window. The smells, the sights, the people, the accent – I oddly had the feeling that I was living in a place I had dreamt about a long time ago.

The apartment was my compensation for teaching at the university. No money exchanged hands.

My duties at the time consisted of teaching two classes at the university, which was only three blocks away. One class was advanced criminal law, in Hungarian. This was the kind of thing I had done in several languages around the world, but in Hungarian it was difficult, teeth-breakingly difficult. But I survived and made some progress, no doubt, in this language that has been challenging me all my life.

The other class was a relief. It was destined for foreign students studying law in Budapest. It turned out that they were virtually all Israelis, Jews and Arabs. In those days, if you did not get into a major university law faculty, you had to go abroad to study. Budapest was closer and cheaper than London. Now the Israelis have developed a chain of private colleges (*michlalot*) that serve the same need the Budapest course served. It is a pity. They need no longer go to Budapest, where they sometimes learned the language and at least received exposure to another culture.

We all used to hang out together at Hanna's Kosher Restaurant on Friday night. Hannah's was located next to the main orthodox synagogue in town and catered to the old folks home as well as the permanent and the wandering orthodox or wannabe orthodox community. We all knew the menu by heart. There was either gefilte fish, beef or chicken, and then some kind of strudel. Everything was cooked in what was assumed to be our collective grandmother's style. The place was mainly an encounter point. Everybody felt free talking to everybody else. Sometimes young travelers came over and told me that I reminded them of their uncle. Would that there were a restaurant like that in New York.

All these experiences made a deep impression on the students as well as on me. Just the other day, as I was walking in the center of Jerusalem, a student stopped me and reminded me that she had been in that class 20 years ago. Also, visiting Hanna's restaurant years later, I ran into a student who married and decided to stay in Budapest.

The Shabbat dinners at a communal Jewish restaurant are one of the advantages of the Eastern European Jewish communities. The number of Jews is small and yet the community is backed by a socialist tradition. The assumption is that someone must organize a Shabbat dinner for the stragglers. Otherwise they would have no place to go. In most places in the US and in the West, no one really cares – except the Orthodox who sometimes issue a general invitation to their homes for a meal for those who live too far to walk home.

There were some other restaurants in Budapest that were my favorites, more because of the food than the others dining there. Tabáni Kakas (The Golden Rooster) is located up on the hill going toward the citadel on the top. They serve the best roast goose in town, and goose is something that Hungarians appreciate with a distinctive national loyalty. We always asked for Pékné mode style, which meant the goose was cut into pieces and mixed with *nookerle* – an Eastern European form of thick dough noodle.

Another place was the Dunakorzó, which was located on the banks of the Danube and serves the best fish soup in the world. When my friend David Brandes was visiting me, he was in a constant trance as a result of the fish soup. They also make a dessert I would be willing to make a special trip to Budapest to enjoy. It is called túrósgombóc. It is a cheese dumpling but made with that special cheese found only in Hungary called túró. Brandes' thespian wife Deena was fascinated by this word and still is. The gombóc (mushroom) came either in sweetened or salted varieties. I generally chose the sweetened coating. It reminded me of the variety some of my aunts made.

Food makes me think of women. Of course, if I had a date, I took her to one of these three restaurants. It turned out, however, that I was more interested in the food than in my dates – with the exception of my current wife Bracha's visit, when I was very concerned about impressing her. Alas, Tabáni Kakas was closed for reparations. But we savored the food at the other two plus a few others we discovered.

During my solitary years in Budapest, women were less important to me than usual. My life was filled with so many sensuous culinary pleasures that I had less concern about whether I would have a partner in bed or not. Perhaps because I did not care, women followed me home all the time. Once a Chinese woman boarded the train with me in Vienna and stuck by my side until we reached my apartment. Another time I met a woman in the countryside while I was cycling. She insisted on coming and spending some time with me overlooking the river.

Once my landlady came in and sat down on my bed to talk to me. I did not respond. She got more provocative and asked whether she made me nervous. I did not quite get it. There were several incidents of that sort. Once one of the more distinguished law professors in town, a single woman, invited me to her home for lunch a deux. I enjoyed the lunch but then came the question: Was I nervous to be alone with her? Actually, I wasn't but I guess I was supposed to be, in light of her intentions. Do not get me wrong. There have been times in my life when I have followed women like a tiger deprived of food for a month. But these were usually when I was frustrated by work or marriage or some other external condition in my life.

Hungarian is the only culture in which the food seems to matter to me so much that it occupies my entire my palate for pleasure. I enjoy every form of cooking – from Japanese to Italian. But none of these has entered my blood stream and created a kind of dependency when the addiction begins in childhood.

## *Politics*

The early 1990s were a time of intense interest in politics – in particular, the transition from state socialism to democratic capitalism. The conflicting parties, including the ruling elite, were engaged in round-table conversations to formulate a non-violent transition. Some of these conversations were bugged. There were scandals. The newspapers were always bursting with headlines. But I did not get much involved until one day a scene presented itself to my balcony on the banks of the Danube. In the last week of October, I began to see traffic jams on the bridges and then I noticed they were taxis and the drivers were leaving them there on purpose. They were clogging the bridges and making car and pedestrian and even bicycle traffic from Buda to Pest impossible. It was a carnival-like scene. I went down among the people and talked to them.

I managed to cross over the Freedom Bridge and gain access to the Gellért Hotel. I went down to the hot baths and sat there seeking conversations with the local bathers about what was going on in the streets. There was a strike, and the people were generally sympathetic. The taxi drivers were protesting the rise in the price of gasoline, caused, I believe by a cutback in the Soviet system of delivering gas to Hungary.

Strikes were something new. They were not allowed under Communism. And they had not yet become so common that they were tedious and boring. There was a great air of excitement. No one knew how it would be resolved. The police declared that they would not intervene. The army would not either. The principle – abused under Communism – was that the army should be held in reserve exclusively for foreign threats. The mood quickly became like a sit-in at an American university in the 1960s. Everyone was having a good time. The people were united, the enemy was big brother.

Then the hardships began. Foreign businessmen could not get to the airport. The borders were closed. Things were getting rough, but the people kept smiling. Finally, a few days into the strike, the parties sat down for a round-table talk and came up with a compromise on the gas increase. It was the best both sides could get. The strike was over, but everyone felt that they had entered a new stage of history. They understood something about the people having power that was only a slogan under the prior regime.

I had always wanted to be part of the anti-DeGaulle riots in the spring of 1968, the *chien lit* – or "dog's bed" as he called them. I was tied down then by teaching duties and was probably too afraid anyway. Participating vicariously in the taxi strike of 1990 was the closest I ever got to the barricades. And even then I enjoyed it all from the comfort of my balcony overlooking the Danube.

There were two other significant legal events in 1990 – both highly symbolic of the transition from state socialism to capitalist democracy. The first was the trial of Joszef Végvári for disclosing official secrets. Végvári had been a member of the secret service before the changeover to democracy. During the intense days of round-table conversations between the socialist and democratic parties, Végvári invited an underground TV crew named *Fekete Doboz* (Black Box) into the secret file chambers of the Hungarian KGB. The cameramen filmed the files of the democratic participants in the round-table discussions and broadcast them on television. Végvári was arrested but soon after that, in February 1990, the democratic forces won the election. The still-serving Communist chief prosecutor refused to prosecute. In his discretionary judgment, he claimed, no harm was done. But then the newly established government appointed a highly principled law professor named Kálman Györgyi as the new chief prosecutor. He analyzed Végvári's crime more abstractly. It is a crime to disclose official secrets, whether the right side benefits or not. He brought a military trial against him. Györgyi was invoking a German principle of prosecution called the Legality Principle. All crime must be prosecuted – there is no room for discretion on behalf of those fighting for the right side.

The trial was fairly straightforward. Végvári was guilty of disclosing state secrets. The most interesting part for me was the verdict issued by the military court. They sentenced him to an "official censure" – the kind of judgment that an organization renders against one of its members. In regular courts the accused is either guilty or not guilty. Judges and juries have no authority to "censure" a free citizen, but internal disciplinary boards claim this power over their "subjects." We shall see in the chapter on English that this problem will recur in the context of a college disciplinary tribunal sanctioning a student rioter.

The third great legal dispute of the time was the Constitutional Court's taking on the issue of capital punishment. All Communist controlled states had maintained the death penalty but many Western states had abolished it and therefore – in contrast to the taxi-strike and the Végvári affair – a decision about capital punishment would be an opportunity to make a statement about Hungary's current political identity. Was it a state bent on becoming Western or not? Once the question is put in this way there is little doubt about the outcome.

The case was brought to the Court under what is called abstract constitutional review. Judicial review in the US requires an actual case or controversy raising the issue, that is, there has to be a real live person threatened by the death penalty for a real crime. The context of the case helps shape our intuitions of justice. In their post-war jurisprudence, however, the Germans introduced the novel idea of abstract review – the Court would have the power to declare a statute null and void simply on the motion of one of the parties defined by law as capable of raising the question. The Hungarians adopted the same principle.

In the Hungarian capital punishment case, the motion to nullify the statute was made by a law professor from Miskolc, a longtime opponent of the penalty. Since there was no case, there were no opposing parties. The court had to proceed by appointing and examining expert witnesses. Of the four who spoke, the most interesting was my friend András Sajó, an academic who often teaches in New York. He appeared to be well-versed in the literature and theory of the death penalty and was to open to considering all arguments for and against.

In contemporary discussions of the death penalty, the argument of retribution rarely gets a fair airing. The argument usually runs: the justification for death must be deterrence and deterrence does not work, therefore the penalty is pointless and in legal terms "arbitrary."

Traditionally, of course, the only argument for capital execution was justice – an eye for an eye – or retribution – *Vergeltung* as Kant formulated the theory. Sajó was on top of all these arguments and offered a sound analysis of retribution as well. The problem always is why long term imprisonment is not sufficient retribution. People rarely remember that Kant wrote before imprisonment was a well-established institution.

I was witness to this excellent academic debate and enjoyed every minute. It was obviously, however, how the matter would come out. After a luncheon break the judges came back and declared the death penalty unconstitutional. They did not have much legal analysis to back them. But these were still revolutionary times. It was clear that the Council of Europe insisted on Hungary abolishing the death penalty, along with other changes in their Soviet-inspired system of criminal procedure. The imperative of the revolution – including joining Western institutions – prevailed over the niceties of legal argument.

On the way out of the courtroom I picked up my coat in the cloakroom. The tag for my hook in the cloakroom had a little inscription on it, to the effect: "Supreme Soviet. Hungarian People's Republic." Old institutions were now serving new purposes.

To be sure, there were other important incidents in the saga of Hungary leaving the Communist orbit and becoming a democratic state integrated into the West. I witnessed the taxi strike, the Végvári case, and the decision to abolish capital punishment. They were typical of the mood in early 1990s.

## *Rackeve*

In the course of this very fertile year, I conceived a program for educating young Eastern Europeans in the basic principles of due process and the rule of law. Working together with a Hungarian activist Kati Koncz, we conceived the name "Raising Rights Consciousness." Funding was easily forthcoming from the National Endowment for Democracy and the Ford Foundation. We found a castle surrounded by a large park on the outskirts of Budapest in a little town called Rackeve. It was perfect for our course. It was located right on the river with a train line to Budapest. Rackeve has but a few attractions, apart from the river. The most important is a good *palacsinta* stand. They served good food in the castle and at night various local bands showed up to play indoors or out and either they danced folk dances or we danced whatever we could improvise. We did this for three summers in a row.

I invited the best people I could – Michael Moore, Heidi Hurd, Meir Dan-Cohen, Elizabeth Warren, Guy Haarscher, Michele Rosenfeld, Robert Post, and even a few judges and practitioners to give the students a feel for the practical side of the law. There was not much else to do so we sat in on each other's courses, so the course became more like a seminar with the professors engaging each other's ideas. The students applied from all over Eastern Europe and were subject to a rigorous selection process. They were uniformly enthusiastic about the experience. Many of them went on to teach in their local law school or to engage in international legal practice. None of us ever forgot those special years on the banks of the Danube River.

Our only problem was that soon we were in competition with the Soros program in the Central European University. We functioned well for three years, but Soros had more money, obviously, and his designs for a permanent institution eventually carried the day.

## *Hungarian or Jewish: Generations Later*

In the great debate between Paul and Frank, there was a sleeper that eventually won the day: Americanization. Neither old-fashioned Judaism nor historic Hungarian culture could hold up against the pressures of the American lifestyle, which pushes us all toward the breakdown of the extended family. People leave home to go to college and then often take jobs on the other side of the country. I remember the year I was visiting at Harvard (1972-73) and I called my mother and said I was not very happy there. I wanted to stay in Los Angeles and be close to her. She replied, "Nonsense, you stay there and become like Kissinger."

Of course, with telephone and email, people who want to stay in touch easily do so. And though I finally did leave LA for the East Coast, I stayed in close touch with my mother. What has disappeared is the Sunday (or Friday night) dinner which you attended – had to attend – simply because you were in town.

I never had any of these ritualized institutions anyway – not even in my nuclear family. There was rarely a family meal of any sort. Rella Berk's memory of living with us in Glendale, when she was a teenager and seeking refuge from asthma attacks in Chicago, was that there was simply a big pot on the stove. When you were hungry you went into the kitchen and took something from the pot. Later, after I was married, a few friends and family – maybe six or eight people – would get together for a Thanksgiving meal. One problem for secularized or Americanized Jews, of course, is that they have no holidays to celebrate. Christmas and Easter are too Christian for all but the converted. The Fourth of July and Labor Day are meaningless. New Year's Eve is dangerous. That leaves Thanksgiving, the only holiday that meant something to me as a child.

In later years we have begun to celebrate family *seders* at Passover and other Jewish holidays, such as Rosh Hashanah and Succot. My older daughter Deborah and her husband Warren keep a Jewish home and send their children, Rachel and Esther, to Jewish schools. My younger daughter Rebecca is a professional cantor and regularly gives multilingual concerts of mostly Jewish music. They are more Jewish than their cousins. No one in their generation speaks Hungarian, but the love of languages has persisted with some. Rebecca has a professional stake in her Hebrew. My cousin Paul, the one time champion of Judaism, spent ten years studying in France and knows both French and German very well.

By and large, however, I look back on the Hungarian immigrants as well as their children and grandchildren as a rich cast of characters that will influence my writing for the rest of my life. In my first novel, *The Bond*, published in 2009, I did not use any of them in the blended characters I created. I relied rather on people I have met in academia, but now I see how indebted I am to these Hungarian Jews, the people who chose to marry them, and their variegated offspring. They were and are a rich crew of eccentrics. By and large, they did not work and still do not work in institutions and therefore they were not forced, as I have been, to smooth down their rough edges.

The men have been sexually unruly. One of them reputedly had a black child on the side in Chicago, but we have never received confirmation of this rumor. He also abused one of our nieces when she was 15 and tried to get it on with Esther, my mother's caretaker. Another is a loner who has never been seen in the company of a man or a woman. A third was a genius of a businessman and could play the violin like a Gypsy without prior training. He also had a keen eye for the ladies and he had the charm that made him irresistible to everyone but his children. A fourth had a deep love of music and managed, despite his limited education, to become a sophisticated connoisseur of opera (and perhaps of women in the music world). Another had a particular weakness for anyone who spoke a foreign language. I am included someplace in this list.

I would not say that the women – particularly my aunts and my sister and their friends – were more conventional but it is more difficult for me to describe my feelings for them. I often felt under their spell. There were times in my early 20s when I looked upon some of the 40ish women with a lust I could hardly conceal. They were taboo in my mind but that did not prevent me from being fascinated by their coquettish and seductive manners of relating to each other and to men. Flora's famous confession, "Georgie boy, a woman has to do..." brought me to her side. I was no longer disturbed by Simone Signore's adultery but felt the thrill of transgression as a way of coping with life.

We call all these people the Rands – even though there is no one still living with the surname Rand. Alex and Harry Rand, the two scions of the family, both died without (known) children, and their wives – also Rands – died shortly thereafter. But the image of Bella Rand stirring her pot of stew with the little ones gathered around her has etched itself in our memory. We carry this woman's power behind us as we emerge as a generation of American lawyers, professors, doctors, and financiers.

Even my cousin Eli, now a student at Penn Law, the son of my youngest cousin Karen (Rand Rubin) who never carried the name Rand, thinks of himself as a Rand. To capture the ability of the women in the family to bear deep grudges, he coined the phrase "Rand rage." I think my grand-niece Lily, daughter of Cheryl, thinks of herself as a part of the Rand clan even though neither she nor her mother Cheryl ever bore the name. Surely, my daughter Deborah and Rebecca think of themselves as Rands. To probe the residues of identity of persons further away in distance and sentiment – Panna and David Lossy in Northern California, I would have to start asking annoying questions. Whatever the degree, the undefined qualify of belonging to a clan is something that still feeds our imagination.

In October 1994, when Rella Berk Lossy was about to die of cancer, she called a Meeting of the Clan at a resort in Northern California. For her, the clan included friends as well as close relatives, as it should have. Weeks later as she lay on her death bed, her son David said to me in tears, "A great spirit is going down, George." We all felt the same way.

I had a similar experience of encountering my clan or a good part of it – though at times more joyful – when I celebrated my 70th birthday last March at the Southernmost House in Key West. I had a few bucks in my savings account, so I invited the senior members of the family in Israel and the USA. A month before the event Bracha and I went down to the Southernmost House and checked out the rooms and made some decisions about who could fit well where – assuming we would have to double up to get everyone in the small hotel and keep the budget down. While we there on that preliminary trip we paid a call on the local T-shirt store, run by a portly transplanted Israeli named Avi. We coined expressions to match the guests and had them blasted on the front of the t-shirt. They all had "Fletch@70" on the back and a personalized touch on the front. One of the more successful was Frank's, dubbed "Head Skipper." Since he is the elder of the family, he is the head but also an avid sailor, thus the second word. The double entendre – Head referring to the John and Skipper someone who skips through the john or "skips" it altogether – makes being the head skipper a little less honorific. His friend and partner Barbara Steinberg was dubbed, "Always in Style" – indeed true about her. They were in the room next to ours, 202 and 201, both with balconies overlooking the southern bay stretching forth to Cuba.

David, Frank's son, a drummer, was on the main level with a room leading to the pool. At some moment in his life he changed his named to Cecil and many in the family call him that. His logo was "Keep the beat." His sister Panna is an M.D. with an adventurous spirit. Her logo read: "M.D. – with a specialization in traveling." Meir bore the log "Not his Student" which only he and I fully appreciated. Meir has followed my work closely over the years but is proud of his never having been officially enrolled in one of my classes. My Israeli cousins had apt if not always funny logos. Shmuel was dubbed "Mr. Fix-it Man" because wherever he is, he takes a peak at what might need fixing. Leah, his wife, received the appellation, "We will save the world – one drink at a time." Leah has a sincere commitment to improving the world, but she also enjoys a good drink and, at most family parties, she is my only drinking partner. Pavla, another cousin from Israel, is a physical education teacher. Her logo read, "Now everyone stretch."

Some of the logos were more successful than others. Rebecca's broadcast "La Estrella" because she is a star and would like to be an even greater one. Deborah had emblazoned on her shirt, "Best Eldest Daughter." Not sure the daughters were amused. My cousin Karen's was "Smooch Sme", which I thought clearly elicited her qualifies as the lovable younger cousin. She did not appreciate that or anything at the party and eventually left – fed up with the demands of family life.

As this chapter begins with Arnold's funeral, it is appropriate to end it with a story of sensuality fulfilled. After a few years alone, Flora met a charming Hungarian Jew named Gene who practiced the ancient craft of transcribing music. His trade has lost out to computer transcription but in the 1980s he still had a strong clientele. His was a dying art – something like the entire set of mannerisms that held our family together. But there was much joy in this wave of late love. When she married Gene, they developed a life of sensuous devotion. They found a place north of San Francisco where they used to go just to enjoy the sun and the pool. They regaled me with stories of their pleasure. It all connects in my mind with the pastry shop on the main street in Nagymihaly, the *cukrasda*, where Harry found the beginning of pleasure in his beloved *krémes*.

## Chapter Five
# Love: Spanish

Despite my promising beginning in the third grade, Spanish acquired negative connotations in my teenage years. It was considered an easy language compared to the German grammar I was studying. Also, it was obvious to me that Spanish was the language of the lower classes in Southern California. It also became the language in which we were likely to talk dirty: ¿Dónde está la casa de la puta? – Where is the house of the whore?" was a phrase I learned before I had the guts to take down my trousers in front of a woman.

One of the rituals of coming of age in LA in those days was racing down to Tiajuana in four hours. Upon piling out of the car, you had to speak Spanish or else. When I was about 16, I met a Mexican whore in the routine course of our roaming the streets south of the border. I paid her the fee, but there was an infant in the room. I took so much pity on her situation – mixed with fear, of course – that my body could not deliver more than a hug. This was the one time in my life that I saw a woman take her panties off one leg, roll them into a ball, and tuck them in under the strap holding them to the other leg. The message to me was clear: Shoot and retreat. Make it fast.

### *Mixed Feelings*

In the context it is hard for me to capture how I eventually developed respect for the Spanish language. The Mexican kids in Southern California did not make it easy for us. You see them in the play *Hair* as Pachukos – zoot-suited sharpies who were much cooler and more violent than anything we could match. In the course of the years they gradually converted into Chicanos, who were more an ethnic group than a gang. Still when the Chicanos zoomed past us in their convertibles – slunk low in the seats – we gasped with fear.

The beach in Santa Monica was the main point of confrontation. Then, as now, there was an amusement park on the pier at the end of Pico Boulevard. The merry-go-round – with hand-carved wooden horses – and a version of the roller coaster have been there as long as I recall. No longer is there the Hall of Mirrors, which as in many places, consisted of a mirror-sided labyrinth where you could easily get lost. In the days when it was still there, a friend of mine and I were wandering through when suddenly, around the corner, a group of Chicanos surrounded us. They taunted and eventually started abusing us – burning live cigarettes into our arms. I was too afraid to fight back. This was not the third grade in Glendale.

It was about this time that I took a rather willful stand against learning Spanish. As a result of my father's wartime import-export business with Géza, there were allegedly some outstanding debts to be paid. The family made a decision to send my sister Lillian on a mission with the necessary cash in her suitcase. (This is apparently the way large sums of money are transferred today between Buenos Aires and the United States). The problem was that she did not know any Spanish. The family looked around among the Hungarian Jews for someone with the talent they needed (it was as though they had a set of yellow pages for Hungarian Jews). They found a Dr. Halmos who, as the story went, ran into some trouble with the law over performing abortions in Chicago and hid out for several years in Santiago, Chile. He learned some kind of Spanish. Lillian went to his home one evening a week for a lesson. My father sent me along – Remember: You are as many persons as languages you speak. But I had no patience for learning Hungaro-Espagnol from the old abortionist and was quickly expelled from the room with instructions to wait quietly by the door.

When I went off to Cornell, I thought I had left behind all the tangents of Spanish culture I had quietly absorbed from the third grade on. No one I knew at Cornell studied Spanish. And the Puerto Ricans – famous for the fight between the Sharks and the Jets – were far away. There were few Blacks. I adopted a Japanese exchange student as my mentee but this was about as exotic an exception as the Jewish boys and Gentile sororities could tolerate. My foreign identities soared off into other directions.

Despite the long latency of my Spanish, Buenos Aires remained in my mind as an alternative reality, as the place where my father could have lived with his brother Géza. The image of Buenos Aires as a kind of shadow home became more poignant about 30 years after the cracking of the piñata in the third grade. We were living in Santa Monica and I was teaching at UCLA. One Friday evening I got a knock on the door. It was not the kind of knock that the Argentines feared in the 1970s, when over 9000 people suspected of being leftist were snatched from their families and made to disappear – sometimes after being tortured. My knocker in 1977 was Jaime Malamud Goti, a criminal law professor from Buenos Aires. He had gone to Berkeley to study the theory of criminal law. The thing he had not anticipated is that criminal law as studied in the United States is an intensely practical subject. He was interested in the highly philosophical version of the subject taught in Germany, Spain, Italy, and Latin America. When no one in Berkeley knew anything about this European version of the subject, he inquired, "Well, who does – at least in California?" "For some odd reason there is a guy in LA," they said, "who knows about this stuff." He gave me a call and I invited him down for dinner.

He arrived on a Friday night, in the middle of a ritualist Shabbat dinner that our family had been practicing for about ten years. The group around the table consisted of my wife Susan, our spiritual leader and future rabbi, then about 37 years old, Deborah, age 13, not terribly interested in the whole thing, and Rebecca, age 9, always very spiritual and destined to become a singer and a professional cantor. Jaime walked onto this stage which must have seemed to him a throwback to a pre-war Polish shtetl – the place from which his father escaped before he landed in Argentina and married a Catholic woman named Goti. Our guest had no idea what to do. In his words, he did not know where to put his feet or his elbows. He suffered through the ritual, enjoyed the dinner, and then as we were cleaning up, in an effort be polite, he blew out the candles. This is a major taboo in Jewish culture. But we did not mind. Jaime had so much charm, such a graceful way with the children, and he could talk shop with me – he had come home in a foreign land called California.

The best we could offer him was the TV room with a linoleum floor and a fold-out bed. The cats hung out there during the day. One was named Lightning. The name of the other has been torturing us for years. Jaime and I had to chase them to get them locked up in the shed out back. If they were not locked up, they would leap up to a second floor balcony and jump on our beds.

During the day Jaime came with me to UCLA, mainly by bicycle, down Wilshire Boulevard, full of 8-10 lanes of traffic and then up through Westwood Village. He took a liking to Herb Morris, my colleague and mentor. The two of us went to Morris's seminar on guilt and shame. Jaime also talked to me about the book on the theory of the criminal law I was then writing. It was called *Rethinking Criminal Law* – the first time anyone tried to write a book covering at least a half dozen different legal systems all with different languages. I tried to cite Spanish sources but the best I could find at the time was the treatise by Jimenez de Asua. Jaime had been his student in Buenos Aires, which gave us a connection through the chains of writing that link – at least in our more metaphysical moments – all the theorists of law in the world.

Jaime is remembered in *Rethinking Criminal Law* in a special way. We had had a discussion about some deep theoretical issue, which can be expressed, in a nutshell, as the way in which we interpret killings in self-defense. The question is: If the law allows you to kill in self-defense, what is the law trying to say to us – that there is a right to kill or that it is merely permitted or tolerated to kill in self-defense? It is a subtle difference, but one that makes European scholars of criminal law dig in their heels. Jaime and I debated this point and he basically convinced me that he was right about the relative prominence of the concept of legal "permission." On page 63, at footnote 27, I thank him for his convincing me that he was right.

The 1970s and early 1980s were hard on liberal lawyers in Buenos Aires. Jaime revealed a sensibility of fear that I have rarely seen in my contemporaries. We were walking one dark night along a side street in Santa Monica when a black sedan pulled up next to us. Jaime jumped for cover. The car was too much like one of those that the agents of the junta used to carry off the *desaparecidos*. It seemed natural for him, however, to go home, remain active in legal affairs, and do whatever he could to bring about change.

The long run of dictatorships in Argentina finally came to an end in the wake of the battles in the spring of 1982 over the Falkland Islands. After the British expeditionary force fought back the Argentine invasion, the military government gave way to democratic elections in October 1983. The transition offered new opportunities to intellectuals like Jaime and Carlos Nino, who were able to contribute their talents to a new legal system. One of their first projects was to organize trials of the generals on various charges of fraud and abuse of power.

In the summer of 1986, Jaime was at the height of his power. I went down to visit him and interview the participants in the trials. Jaime had been a close personal advisor of President Alfonsin who was elected as the head of the Radical party. But he always had the boyful charm that endeared him earlier to my daughters. One night he gave me a special show, which involved his making a sneak entry with his .45 drawn. These were dangerous times, particularly when the enemy was then the army and they had the weapons. But for Jaime it was all good for laughs.

We were driving down the broad boulevard called Santa Fe and we passed the Naval Academy, which became famous when Jacob Timmerman published his book about being tortured there. A sign declared boldly that it was illegal to stop in front of the academy. The terrifying implication was that a stopped vehicle would be destroyed on the spot. This was not very funny.

Among my many interviews, two stand out in my mind. One was with an ambitious, handsome young assistant prosecutor with a thick black beard. He is still handsome, still prosecuting, still with a thick beard, though now slightly greyed. His name is Luis Moreno Ocampo, now the chief prosecutor of the International Criminal Court in the Hague. The other was a member of the Communist Party named David Baegun. He had a leftist interpretation of the prosecutions. They stood in his mind for the revolution of the working class.

There was something profound about the trials and maybe "revolution" was a good approximation of their social meaning. As I began to interpret the events years later, they came to stand for the first systematic victory of a new movement in criminal justice – the victims' movement. The critical force behind the prosecutions was the prolonged period of marching in the streets by the *madres* and the *abuelas* – the mothers and grandmothers of the disappeared. Their haunting presence – carrying pictures of their kidnapped children – was too much for any government to resist.

When other victims' groups made their voices heard in the US – gays, Blacks, Jews, raped women – their implicit model was the mothers who cried for their children in Buenos Aires. Interviewing the various players in the trial was the first hard practical work I had to do in Spanish. I loved every minute of it. The friendship with Jaime led me to the important people. We even had a lunch scheduled especially for the judges of the Supreme Court, Jaime and myself. I found it peculiar that Jaime, as a representative of President Alfonsin, had easy access to the judges. I think there are similar forms of communication between the executive and the judiciary in the US, but we do not hear much about them. The odd thing is that I never published anything about my experiences, but as will become evident, I have had major legal experiences in most of the seven languages under discussion and I have never published anything about them. For purposes of my career as a legal scholar, I have concentrated on philosophical problems in the law. This is the occasion for me, not only to reflect on my life in seven languages, but also on these trials that fell below the threshold of philosophical relevance. For most people, the tales of these trials – including the hijackings in Germany and the Soviet Union – would probably prove more interesting than the theoretical work I learned to do in German.

## *Activism*

The trip to Buenos Aires in 1986 came at a time in my life when my interests had already begun to turn to the impact of the law on ordinary people. Another trial – not ostensibly linked to the Spanish language – brought me closer than I expected to this language, which is now so important to me. In December 1984, a young man named Bernie Goetz shot four young Blacks on the New York subway. With pre-trial procedures taking a year and a half, the highest court of New York finally decided in the same summer of 1986 that the case would finally go to trial. My decision to attend the trial and to write a book about the case led to an unexpected and very intense intersection with Spanish legal culture.

The first stage was attending the trial and writing the book itself. *A Crime of Self-Defense* was an original venture. Though there have been some great books about trials, this was the first time anybody had written a theoretical take on a particular trial that included everything from jury selection to oral argument. This was possible only because I attended the trial and it happened to be in a field – namely self-defense – in which I had already published hundreds of pages. The book appeared in 1988 and received a bit more publicity than most of my books, which are usually treated as academic texts. The Goetz book surfaced in many bookstores where casual buyers could stumble upon it. One such casual buyer was a professor of criminal law from Seville, Spain, Francisco Muñoz Conde, known to everyone close to him as Paco. He noticed the book in the Harvard Coop when he was in Cambridge visiting his son.

One day I got a call from Paco, much like the call from Jaime more than a decade earlier. The point was the same. The caller was 400 miles north of my home. He wanted to come down and talk to me, this time to New York instead of Los Angeles. Paco arrived at my apartment on May Day, 1989. We quickly came to an agreement which I had no reason at all to oppose. He wanted to translate my book into Spanish and introduce it into the Spanish-speaking world. Though I had been publishing books for over a decade, this was the first time that someone wanted to take my ideas and import them into a different legal culture. We signed no contract and indeed I had no basis for investing my trust in Paco's capacities as a translator. He had not translated anything from English before, but for that matter, so far as I knew, no one had translated a book about law from English into any other language.

Would that it were not trite to comment that Paco was discovering a new world like the Spanish explorers before him. In fact, Paco's project, beginning with that casual conversation in my living room at 404 Riverside Drive, New York, was a major event in European-American legal understanding. He began with the Goetz book, which came out a year or so later as *La defensa propia*, then he started on my other books – *Conceptos basicos de derecho penal, Las victimas ante el jurado, Loyaltad.* As fast as I could write, Paco would translate. Truth to tell, I have lost track of all his translations. In the introduction to one of my recent books, *The Grammar of Criminal Law*, published in 2007, I thank Paco twice for translating my books. Once I mentioned that the number of translations is three (p. xvi of *The Grammar*) and a few pages later I give the number as "seven or eight" (p. xx of the same). The truth is someplace in between.

The number of translations is not nearly as important as the way Paco devoted his time to introduce the ideas of his translations into Spanish legal discourse. Every time he published a new translation, he invited me to come to Spain to travel to different universities and to give a series of lectures about the book. We discovered in the course of these long car trips that we had much in common. We had the same birthday: March 5 (though I was a few years older). We both had a child born out of wedlock. We both loved Brecht's *Die drei Groschen Oper* – The Three Penny Opera – which he played over and over again as we zoomed through the plains of Andalusia. We both tried to speak Japanese, but not very well. Once Paco got out of the car to make a call to Japan from a street phone in some wayward village, let's call it Ubeda. He carried on the conversation in Japanese and explained that he was with me and that we were speaking Japanese. Then when he resumed driving he made up the joke: Yes, all the women in Japan are trying to figure out who are these two Japanese-speaking guys in Ubeda. The word is now out. It's Paco and Fletcher.

Paco was capable of enormous dedication and concentration. He made a decision to introduce Anglo-American ideas about criminal justice into Spain and nothing was going to stop him. Part of this commitment stems from his political background. He was a staunch enemy of Franco, the Church, Opus Dei – all the forces that held back Spain as an economy and as a culture several decades behind France and Germany. German ideas were not entirely new in Spanish culture but as Paco showed in much of his courageous later work, many of the German writers of the period were still tainted by ideas on the social control of deviants developed under National Socialism. Spain and the rest of Europe were in a rut of repeating old ideas. Bring in the American ideas of the jury and adversary systems, the rules of evidence, the principle of utilitarian or cost/benefit thinking, prosecutorial discretion, jury nullification – these were ideas that forced Europeans to think anew about their legal systems. Obviously, not everything the Americans had to export was good but it was worth discussing, just as the reverse is true for Americans.

Paco's point was not didactic. He simply wanted Spaniards to become familiar with the idea of criminal justice that prevailed in a country that could not be ignored in world politics. What made my work acceptable to Europeans is that I had shown in everything I had written since 1978 that I knew their system well and that therefore the conversation was among friends, scholars who shared common ground.

The publisher was always Tiran lo Blanc in Valencia, which apparently gave Paco carte blanche to publish whatever he wanted. The amiable editor Anton Vives always greeted me in the course of my trips in Spain and gave me an envelope of cash to cover my expenses.

The side benefit of our traveling and lecturing around Spain is that I learned Spanish. I would write a lecture in English, Paco would translate it into Spanish, and then I would read it in a half dozen different places around Spain. Also, I had to function in the dinners afterward – I needed to know enough Spanish to make it clear to the waiters that I did not eat pork or shell fish and to implore the other guests not to smoke in my face. The latter request infuriated Paco because smoking was then commonplace in Spanish restaurants and sometimes after our day's work, I would go back to the hotel and light up a cigar. He did not understand that cigar smokers often cannot stand the smell of cigarette smoke and vice versa.

With each trip I got better and eventually could speak impromptu and field questions in Spanish from the audience. Of course my vocabulary was limited. But this is a principle for learning languages worth keeping in mind – learn to speak about a specific subject. It does not matter what it is, criminal law, cars, cooking, fancy suits or sewing. If you keep your range of discourse limited, you will internalize the structure of the sentences that you have to use over and over again.

### *Bracha*

Buenos Aires gradually transformed itself from a city of my imagination into a place on the ground where I know addresses, places to visit, friends to see, little cafes and shopkeepers who greet me with warmth and familiarity. Jaime was the first step of my absorption into the life of the city. Even more important was my exposure and enthusiasm for tango. I first learned the Argentine Tango on a very shaky dance floor in the hold of a cruise ship heading for Valparaiso, Chile. I was on that ship largely because of my fortuitous role as a TV commentator on famous criminal trials in the late 1980s and early 1990s. These years, which lasted from the Goetz trial in 1987 to the O.J. Simpson marathon-TV series in 1995, became an unusual period in American pop culture. The lay viewers wanted to learn about how criminal trials worked; professors and other lawyers became valued, typically as non-paid guests on shows with hosts like Geraldo, one of the many who became famous because of their coverage of crime and justice. Some of the early guests like Roger Cossack and Nancy Grace developed shows of their own. It was a boom that converted a bunch of lawyers into stars for a day.

I became one of these lawyerly kibitzers, satirized beautifully in a little routine by Billy Crystal: As the elevator operator, he calls out the floors as the elevator descends floor by floor into the lower depths of hell. Fourth level of hell – the insurance salesman get out; the fifth level down – time for the auto mechanics to exit – by the time we descend to the eighth or ninth level, the elevator operator announces, "All lawyers who comment on TV trials get out here."

Billy Crystal had it right. We were essentially carpetbaggers striving for a little attention because the public was hungry to hear about criminal trials. The side benefit of being one of these instant experts is that the public thinks of you as a mini-star – at least for a season or two. Lots of benefits flow to mini-stars. In my case the benefit was a free trip – in fact two free trips on Cunard Lines – from Florida to Chile. All I had to do was give three lectures about these famous cases while on board, and the whole thing was free. It was a good gig. The only downside was that we all got a little bored. The beneficial consequence was that we were invited to sign up for activities like tango lessons.

It turned out that I love to dance and in particular the tango, which is not so rigorous rhythmically as the salsa or the other Latin dances. You can set your own pace and after you learn the basic steps, you can make up your own dance patterns. The trick for the man is learning how to lead, and for the woman, how to follow. For several years thereafter I danced tango wherever I could – in Jerusalem, in Paris, in the mountains in Northern Italy, in New York. In a moment of zeal I started saying that my citizenship was USA, my nationality was Jewish, and my religion was tango. Interestingly, I did not say anything about my languages.

Inevitably, however, tango brought me closer to Spanish. First, just about all of the teachers are Argentines. Second, the language of the dance and all of the music – from Gardel to Piazzola – is Argentine. You cannot learn the steps without picking up a dozen news words from *crusada* to *gancho*. In the early 2000s I started taking trips to Buenos Aires just to dance. I would stay at Jaime's place and find the local milongas and dance. It was perfectly acceptable to show up alone at these milongas and ask any woman you fancied to dance. Sometimes they would say no by not looking up to notice you but generally they would say yes. In fact, it was rather easy to get the idea that local ladies were attracted to the tourists who showed up at these communal dances. But then I discovered that most of the ladies who were thrilled to dance with me were in fact teachers of the art. They started out by being very complimentary and then saying something like, "If you want to really get good, here is my card, give me a call."

It was clear, however, that trying to pick up women at dance classes or milongas was bad form. Even the routine practice of cheek to cheek dancing was not a come on. It was just the accepted style of dancing. Names were rarely exchanged, and though sometimes the newly acquainted left together, it was not the pattern. Of course I had thought how wonderful it would be to meet a woman who also loved to dance tango. Then, to adapt the French expression, everything would be perfect – *a piste et au lit* – on the dance floor and in bed. Actually the French regard the table as more important than the dance floor, thus the real expression is *tout est bien a table et au lit*. I once confessed this desire of double perfection, as adapted to tango, to a woman I was dancing with on a Sunday afternoon on the wooden docks boarding the East River in Manhattan. She replied in a sultry voice, "This is what we all dream about." Of course it was not so easy. Dancers are peculiar types. Many are drawn to the floor precisely because they do not have the social skills to support a date over wine and dinner. I did not think I was one of these, but you can never be sure.

In October 2005, when I took one of my trips from New York to BA just to dance, I also had "meeting someone" on my mind. Jaime did not really know any tango dancers so his girlfriends fixed me up with an artist. We went for dinner, all together, in Spanish of course. She kept nudging her friend and asking, "*El entiende? El entiende?*" – Does he understand? Does he understand? Of course, I understood – more than she realized. One of the things that I understood is that it is not easy for people to relate to foreigners who are less than perfect in their native language. I have been doing it all my life – none of my older relatives spoke perfect English. But I understand the intolerance of those who are more isolated among native speakers. I have a similar feeling of impatience when I have to listen to someone speaking a broken form of any of my adopted languages, that is, any except English.

As I returned home to New York, I did not realize that the gears were already in motion that would radically alter my romantic life and enable to feel *tout est bien a table et au lit.* Paco came to Buenos Aires the following month to give one of his frequent lectures (I should add here that for many years Paco's journeys resembled those of the Jewish merchants of the Middle Ages. He brought the news from one place to another. He provided the bond that linked all of us in the academic field of criminal law together). He met one of his old friends Sandra Eugeni and mentioned to her that I had just been in Buenos Aires and it was a pity that Jaime did not introduce us. He was sure we would hit it off. I am sure that was a better bet than with the artist who was preoccupied by the question, "El entiende?" Jaime seemed to think I would be coming back to BA very soon.

For the next several months Sandra and I were engaged in a symbolic long distance tango. I would make a move in one direction – say to California – then she would go north to Bahia in Brazil. I holed up in my hotel room writing a brief for the Supreme Court; Sandrita went outside to enjoy the beach in Bahia. Then I had to go to Turkey to give a lecture, she returned to Buenos Aires and inquired after me. No news so she wrote me an email. I went off email for the entire three weeks I was in Turkey. The message downloaded into my inbox but in the course of my travels I had no access to the internet and I had no idea that a life-changing message was waiting for me. Finally I arrived in Israel but at the Mishkenot HaSha'anim – an elegant residence for scholars – I had no access either. They had their own computers for which – it is hard to believe this today – you had to pay by the hour. My inadvertent isolation finally ended when I moved in my new house, one that I had purchased six months before and appropriately had arranged for phone service with wireless internet throughout the house.

It took me a couple of weeks to get the house painted and ready for moving in and buy the minimal furniture necessary for sleeping and eating. Just at that moment I had to return to New

York to give a lecture to the graduate students. I passed by the house and checked my email, finding two replies from Sandrita to my messages, the first written before my trip to Turkey and the other, when she was slightly annoyed not to find a response to her first. I responded back immediately but did not have a chance to call until I hit New York a few days later. Interestingly we wrote in English, but from the first conversation by telephone we spoke in Spanish.

In any relationship where a choice of language is possible, the first conversation is critical. Once the language is established you cannot change it. Both sides become conscious of other languages being artificial. I have discovered this to be true with many friends and now I was about to establish the same principle with the woman who two years later would become my wife.

Our first meeting in person occurred in April 2005. One of my favorite students in criminal law, Luis Ernesto Chiesa Aponte, whom I call by his acronym LECA, had invited me to San Juan, Puerto Rico, to give a lecture at the law school. I lectured on the Hamdan case, the one on which I had written the brief in Los Angeles, and which had just been heard by the Supreme Court. By this time Sandra – or she was now called Bracha – and I were almost lovers, though we had never met in person.

And how did Sandra become Bracha? In one of our first conversations, we both noticed that I kept referring to her in Spanish as *mi bendición, mi bendición,* my blessing, my blessing. She asked me how to say that in Hebrew. The translation is *bracha*. "Good," she said, "that is my name." It has been ever since. Whether Barack Obama's first name has the same origin is a matter of some dispute. The better wisdom seems to be yes, it is simply the Arabic equivalent. The alternative theory is that it derives from the name Barak, who is a prominent figure in the book of Judges. In any event, acts of naming are decisive events. And this one reoriented us from the Spanish to the Hebrew language.

Yet the Spanish language remained our intimate private

idiom that virtually no one around us (in Jerusalem at least) understands. I credit myself with a little piece of wisdom about language and power in male/female relationships. In our case the issue is particularly delicate. We are both lawyers. Bracha was a litigating corporate lawyer for 20 years in Buenos Aires before she met me. She could not tolerate anything but a relationship of full equality. My instinct at the outset was that I was likely to have issues over power with her as I have had with other women. So I tried something new. I ceded her the language at the outset. She is more competent in Spanish than I am, which means she has a natural power advantage. She could misuse it, which many people do, by laughing at the mistakes of the person weaker in the language. (*El entiende*? *El entiende*?) But she never does. She shows me that she has the power but that she respects me regardless of my mistakes. I am sure that this contributes to our very successful relationship and since November 28, 2007, our successful marriage.

Of course physical attraction is not to be underestimated in any successful loving relationship, and no less in ours. From the first time we saw each other in the Miami airport we could not keep our hands off each other. In my mind this attraction cannot be totally separated from the love affair I had in mind for many years with Buenos Aires and eventually for the Spanish language. Some places, for some people, simply reek with erotic pull. The music, the rich dark color of Latin skin, the typically thick straight black hair, the tango, the way she moves and looks at me – this is enough to make me predisposed to love. As someone once told me, in some other language, when the physical attraction is present, it represents about 10% of the relationship. When it is absent, it casts a spell over 90% of what you have. In other words, if you have it, you have to start working; if you don't have it, the situation is hopeless.

With all these concessions to conventional wisdom, allow me to dwell on Bracha's beauty – lithe, trim, elegantly dressed, black hair combed straight back – and in particular the scene she presented on our first trip from the Miami airport to Key Largo. I did my part by renting a red convertible. Picture the two of us – the slightly aging Jewish college professor and the young sexy fashionable Latina – barreling down Highway One. Well I am not sure if anyone noticed, but I did and I loved what I saw. The Florida Keys themselves are among the most romantic places on the planet, with their combination of exotic vegetation, haphazard building, manicured ocean views and accidental land masses. We both fell hopelessly in love. We still know the exact spot in the Miami airport where we parted with tears on our final day.

Our relationship was realized by many trips back and forth among the ports of Buenos Aires, New York, and Jerusalem. Each of these places has an appeal and each is a home to us. In Buenos Aires we have Jaime, his friend and mine Juancho, Bracha's father Francisco, her two sisters, a niece and nephew, and many cousins I have never met. We are comfortable either in the apartment that Bracha bought with her own earnings as a lawyer (something that impressed me) or in the luxurious extra apartment that Jaime recently acquired. We have found our favorite tango studio on the corner of Santa Fe and Callao and a teacher to whom we are devoted, Elsa Maria, whose photographs show her dancing with visitors Bill Clinton and Shimon Peres.

In New York, we live in a glorious apartment with four large rooms overlooking Riverside Drive. The environment is obviously friendly to both Spanish and English-speakers. Columbia Law School has provided me with an excellent position as a Cardozo Professor of Jurisprudence. Between these two places we have all that we could want, but the life of the heart has it own rhythms. On one of our trips I came to the view that the best home for us is a place we both love but where neither of us is completely rooted, namely Jerusalem, in the house I bought five years ago on a street called "Lovers of Zion." Bracha immediately agreed and we moved there in December 2006. Spanish is still our language but we are surrounded every day by Hebrew and to a lesser extent by Russian and English.

*Bracha and George, in Jerusalem, with the Old City in the background.*

The street on which we live has great significance for us because the great Romantic philosopher Martin Buber lived here – only about five houses down the block. He was a key figure in our exploring each other's spiritual selves. When Bracha heard that Buber lived right down the street and that his spirit was still felt in the neighborhood, we found a copy of *I and Thou* in Spanish and started reading it to teach other. The fundamental idea of Buber's philosophy is that personal relationships – instantiated by addressing the other as Du or Thou – differed categorically from our way of relating to things – to objects that we call "it." Power struggles in human relationships are always characterized by one side's trying to treat the other as an object of will. The idea of an "I and Thou" relationship is not power but interpersonal recognition – the meeting of the other in a space defined by two spirits seeking to engage.

I wish we could claim Buber for the Spanish language. But of course Buber belongs to the greats of German philosophy. Yet as I have discovered from Buber and other readings, Spanish offers

*Bracha, in Jerusalem, at the Western Wall.*

many advantages for expressing theological ideas. One of the minefields for those seeking to translate the Hebrew text of the Bible into English is the entire field of pronouns – the ways of referring to persons as masculine, feminine or neuter. Many of the misunderstandings of the English translations of Genesis are a consequence of innate restrictions in the use of the pronouns. The distinction between Yo and Tu, Ich and Du, is clearer than the English improvision of Thou as the equivalent of the second person intimate. Ordinary English fails us by relying on "You" for all relationships, whether intimate or distant. Also, as in other Romance languages, the possessive pronoun in the third person *su* agrees in gender with the thing possessed. In English, German, and Russian, the pronoun – his or her – agrees with the gender of the possessor. The shift in the referent makes it easier to translate some biblical passages without slipping into the mistake of using the masculine possessive "his" and thus treating God, falsely, as male. I explore this and related themes further in the chapter on Hebrew.

As in the case of Hungarian, the formal grammar tells us little about the sexism of the society. Latinos have their own special way of defining the power and attraction of women, and in my view they have a very successful solution to this problem

*Bracha and George, in New York.*

that trips up so many people. Women are equal in the workplace. Several presidents in Latin American have recently been women (Michelle Bayelet in Chile, Christina Kirschner in Argentina). This and other successes of women have not compromised the extraordinary gift of Latin women to dress attractively and to radiate warmth in their business and personal relationships.

By bringing together these theological and personal reflections, I feel that I have come full circle. I am back in the third grade visiting the Spanish missions in Southern California. I am in the spiritual world that Bracha and I have developed alongside our physical longings. I have brought the Buenos Aires of my childhood imagination into union with the circuit of my travels and residences. The life of childhood fantasy has joined with the daily project of building a successful marriage. All of this has happened in the Spanish language, and it is but one of the seven languages we have had to consider in the life of a person who thinks of himself as a unified whole.

Chapter Six

# My People: Hebrew

When I started college, the last thing on my mind was learning Hebrew or seeking to educate myself about the Bible and Judaism. My loyalties at the time were directed more toward Hungary than Israel. I recall that in 1952, in the eighth grade, I was enormously proud to be a wannabe Hungarian because Hungary took third place in the 1952 Olympics. It had strong gymnastic and fencing teams. For both Hungary and Israel, 1956 was a big year. That was my first semester at Cornell and my two countries were the two "little giants" in the news. Both had engaged in heroic ventures. The Hungarians tried to pull off their revolution in October 1956 and the Israelis invaded the Sinai, with the help of the British and the French. All of a sudden I felt at the center of world politics.

My father's reactions to these two events of 1956 were significant for me. He had disdain for the Hungary Revolution. He thought it was run by fascists and his proof was that the Cardinal Mindszenty, whom he probably associated with the anti-Semites of his youth, took refuge in the American embassy. On the other hand, the Israel campaign into Sinai awakened his Jewish pride. He called my attention to the young Jewish soldiers he saw on the front page of the Los Angeles Times. I understood this. For post-Holocaust observers, the heroic Jewish soldier was a new phenomenon. Suddenly, my father was in touch with yearnings that had been suppressed since the time he left Hungary during its plague of anti-Semitism in 1919.

The excitement of the fall 1956 tapered off and I was stuck with commitments in student politics. This was not good for my studies and it took me several years to extricate myself. Eventually I settled down as a student and nothing much happened in my Jewish life. In those years I never went to services, never attended a Shabbat dinner, never ate a certified kosher meal, never attended a *seder*. I was about as assimilated as a teenager could be. Oddly though, all my friends were Jewish. The social bonds remained after everything else melted away.

My closest friend in those days was Gerald Goldfarb. He lived across the hall from me in the freshman dorms and he volunteered to be my campaign manager when I ran for Freshman Class President. He lived on Avenue M in Brooklyn. Visiting him and his family in a real Jewish neighborhood was an adventure for me. I was impressed by his uncle, who stood up at the Thanksgiving table and gave a touching speech. This was not exactly a Jewish performance but I had never seen anything like it in the self-conscious and embarrassing events that passed as rituals in my home.

### *Arthur Lagawier*

Nothing changed in my Jewish life until I spent a year in Germany in 1964-65. As I have already described, that year I had a sudden awakening of Jewish consciousness – provoked by living among Germans so soon after the war. After returning to the United States, Susan and I found a wonderful offbeat rabbi named Arthur Lagawier, one of the greatest influences on my life. He was an idiosyncratic man full of charm. An immigrant from Holland, he was learned in Talmud as a child and never gave up his love for the books, even though he made a living as a jeweler. He studied Talmud every morning but so far as I know he never found a group he felt comfortable praying with. He befriended us and invited us to my first Shabbat dinner.

He had a very interesting theory about the Ten Commandments, which I will take the liberty of explaining briefly here. Apparently no one has ever been convinced by his theory, so I feel a debt to my teacher to make his theory more widely known to the world. The word for "do not" in the Ten Commandments in Exodus 22 is *Lo*. *Lo Tignov* means "Do not steal." The curious thing about this is that in speaking Hebrew, you would express the point differently, you would say *Al Tignov* for "Do not steal." So why is there this discrepancy? *Lo* is generally used to indicate the future, so *Lo Tignov* should mean "You will not steal." *Lo* has this connotation in all places, except in the common interpretation of the Ten Commandments. Lagawier's point was that everyone had read the Ten Commandments incorrectly. They were really predictions about how you would behave if you accepted the first commandment, which is the affirmation of God's role in history. Therefore, the famous ten are not imperatives at all. They are not orders. They are not laws. They are predictions about how you will behave if you accept God and build your life around your faith. Significantly, in Hebrew, they are not called commandments, even though the religion is oriented toward its 613 commandments. The famous passage in Exodus is called the Ten Words. I think Lagawier was probably right. His teaching resonated with me.

Within a few years we had faced an existential test about being Jews. In the Six Day War of 1967, I felt that my own life – along with the State of Israel – was on the line. If Israel had been destroyed, I would have been destroyed. I cannot explain this feeling except as a culmination of other exposures to Judaism that I describe in this chapter. I recall staying glued to the radio in our kitchen in Seattle. After an intense experience of that sort something would have to change. We had to take our Jewish lives more seriously.

Susan and I had a chance to visit Israel in 1962 when we took our honeymoon trip through Europe. We got as far as Greece, but Israel "seemed" too far. Sometimes our actions express beclouded rationalizations we barely understand.

But how would we correct this mistake? We now had two children. It was not so easy to pick up and travel to Israel, and what would I do there? We had a lucky break a year or two later. The former dean of the law faculty in Jerusalem, Shalev Ginossar, came to Seattle on a trip around American universities to promote the cause of Israel and his university. He was a Belgian scholar who had written a book in French about the theory of private law. Fortunately, I had found the book in our library before he came and I had read it. He was very impressed and we became instant friends. He was resolved to get me to Jerusalem one way or another.

It turned out not to be hard. We moved to UCLA shortly thereafter in 1969 and one of the first projects the local rabbi, Richard Levy, announced, with the support of the American Jewish Committee, was a program to send all Jewish faculty who had never been to Israel on a two-week seminar in the country to study its every aspect. I could not have been more thrilled. My traveling companion and roommate from UCLA was Bob Gerstein, a lawyer and political scientist. The rest of the group came from universities all over the country. With our impressive guide Gahlia Golan (originally Gail Green) we traveled around the country and saw everything worth our minds' attention. Every morning we had an intellectual seminar with some of the leading scholars in Israel. They were mostly philosophers or political scientists, a first-rate lineup. I was already studying Hebrew because I remember showing up for breakfast with the list of words I had to memorize for that day.

The seminar had the best possible effect on me. I found myself at home with a bunch of Jewish intellectuals – the students and the professors. Even more surprising, Ginossar had arranged a meeting with his colleagues in the law school, and I found to my great surprise that many had read my first major article which appeared in 1967 in the Yale Law Journal. They loved it. It was comparative law. It was analytic. It was rigorous. It revealed the knowledge of several languages. It was exactly their style. The dean hinted that they would invite me to come for a visiting appointment in 1972-73. The invitation was not made formal until the new dean Zalman Feller took over. He was a criminal lawyer like myself – from Romania, with a weak knowledge of English. Therefore he insisted on one condition that I was pleased to accept. He said I had to teach in Hebrew. In those days Western scholars did not come and teach in English. The Zionist spirit was still so strong that newcomers were expected to learn Hebrew. And besides, he wanted to understand what I was telling "his" students. Also, the dean was right on one important point. I would not develop a lasting tie to Israel without learning the language.

### *Jerusalem, 1972-73*

The family was excited about joining me in this great adventure. Deborah would enter the third grade, Rebecca, kindergarten. They were both beautiful schools in the neighborhood of Rehavia, though for various reasons neither exists today. With the help of a Hungarian-speaking friend who also claimed to be a likely relative, Yehuda Blum, we found a large well-furnished apartment on a quiet street in the center of Rehavia. It was Shlomo Molcho 1. My mother convinced my niece Cheryl to come with us to spend her junior year in Jerusalem. The Hebrew University has a special course in English for third year students. So there were five of us in the spacious apartment. We were in a very nice position to invite people over and we ourselves were invited very often. Life was more social then. The standard invitation was for coffee and cake on Shabbat afternoon. These were wonderful events where I got to know my colleagues and their families.

The part that was not so easy was that in order to learn Hebrew, I had to insist on speaking Hebrew to everyone, everywhere. There was a precedent for this kind of obstinance. Eliezer Ben Yehuda, who is credited with reviving modern

Hebrew in the early 20th century, also had the practice of speaking only Hebrew with everyone he met in what was then called the Yishuv – the settlement prior to the State of Israel. Of course, communication would have been more efficient for Ben Yehuda in German or English but that was not the point. Language has great ideological significance, though it is not so easy to explain what it is. We define ourselves as a community by speaking a language and knowing that total strangers also speak the language. This was the great insight of Benedict Anderson in his book *Imaginary Communities*. The point is not that communities are just invented as fictions, but that they exist first and foremost in our minds. If we can speak to other people, even potentially speak, or just read what they have written or have them read to us, we are tied by a special bond across space and time.

Speaking Hebrew in Israel was a way of making a statement about the kind of state Israel should be. It should be a community, whether secular or religious, tied to the Bible. There was a big debate at the Technion in the first decade of the 20th century about whether the language of instruction should be German or Hebrew. German was then the dominant language of science. It was the rational choice. Hebrew was for the ideologues, the nationalists, the Romantic Zionists. They prevailed. Note that this theory, unfortunately, leaves no room for the large minority of Arabic speakers in Israel.

I once asked my friend Meir Dan-Cohen, who grew up in Israel, but lives in the US and considers himself a totally emancipated intellectual, free of allegiance to the Bible, what he would have decided at the Technion: German (or English) or Hebrew. He thought for a few minutes and then said, "Hebrew." The choice has no plausible rationale except the nationalist argument that Hebrew would revive sentiments of national identity.

When I arrived in Israel I followed the model of Ben Yehuda (as noted earlier, I have followed this model in several languages). When I first presented myself to the law faculty, I spoke to them in broken Hebrew. Even though I knew about five sentences when I arrived, I had to use these and add to them when I could or there was no hope. The biggest problem was that educated Israelis were delighted to practice their English and therefore switched to English whenever they could – except if they noticed – ironically – that a foreigner wanted to enter the conversation. Then they would always speak Hebrew. One of my colleagues, a brilliant man who spoke Russian very well and lived up the street from me on Shlomo Molcho, invited us for dinner. But he had no patience for my broken Hebrew, so the condition of the invitation was that we had to speak English. I politely declined. I had little contact with him after that.

From the time we arrived in early summer 1972, I had four months before the beginning of the fall term. The dean kindly appointed a private tutor to help me (I have never gotten past the basics of a language in a formal class). His name was Reuven Bar Chaim. He became my shadow, following me around, explaining this or that point of grammar to me. He came to my classes and wrote down my mistakes. He filled me with enthusiasm for the language. Alas, the last time I saw him, he was recovering from a cancer operation.

Another great influence at the time was Bob Cooper. I met him and his family on a hike organized by the alumni of the university. Also an American academic, his field was socio-linguistics and he also taught at the Hebrew University. He heard me speaking Hebrew on the hike and asked me how long I had been in the country. When I said a couple of months, he decided that I was a case worthy of scientific investigation. He invited me over to his beautiful apartment in the Bauhaus building opposite the Bezalel School of Art in the center of Jerusalem. He had the most fantastic artwork which he and his wife Alice had brought with them after a year in Ethiopia. This is a man I admire, I immediately thought to myself.

He also admired me, so we had an easy basis for a friendship. He stayed in Israel while I continued to go back and forth. He was not a Zionist, he said, it was just the best job he could find. He retired at age 60 and set out, alone, to traverse the globe by land and sea. He kept a diary and generated a charming manuscript about his personal adventures, but could not find a publisher. Then he wrote a very clever book about Mark Twain's world tour in 1895. He repeated the tour in 1995 and wrote about the changes over time. That is the kind of idea you need to write a good travel book.

I remember the day I opened the International Herald Tribune someplace in Italy and found a review of *Around the World with Mark Twain*. I called him immediately. Now he is working on a book on the 1835 fire in New York City. We spoke English together but his recognition gave me great support in my struggle to master Hebrew.

## *My Israeli Family*

At the level of my grandparents, the family split into the Rand and the Blau factions. The Rands went to live in the US and the Blaus came to Israel. Esther Blau married Zev Kraus and they lived for a while on a Czech-speaking Kibbutz named after the nation's first president, Tomáš Masaryk. Because of the timing of their exodus, namely they left at least a decade later than my family, they thought of themselves as Czechs rather than Hungarians.

My mother felt a great attachment to Esther Blau. I too made several trips to visit her in Tivon near Haifa, where they lived after leaving the Kibbutz The personal affection between Esther and my mother passed on to the next generation. My two cousins from Tivon, Shmuel and Pavla, more or less of my generation, eventually moved to Jerusalem and married, respectively, Lea and David and had five children. The children have already generated six grandchildren, four living in Jerusalem and one in Tel Aviv. We have become close to all of them. That Bracha and I speak Hebrew with them has become a major plus. And the surprising thing – I think that relatives are always a gamble – is that they are very interesting people and greatly enrich our lives.

The story of relatives on my father's side is more complicated. His two brothers and one sister, Amál, went to live in the southern cone of Latin America. I don't why they moved to places close and yet far from each other. Géza went to Buenos Aires. Marci and Amál went to Santiago, Chile. Amál eventually migrated from Chile to Israel with her son. The story was that she left Chile in some kind of scandal. I assumed that the scandal was that she gave birth out of wedlock, and that therefore her name was still Fleischer, the same as my father's before he changed it. When my mother came to visit us in 1972, during my first stint as a visiting professor at the Hebrew University, she took a taxi and went north to visit Amál and presumably her son. The fate of Amál and her son is still clouded.

Once I tried to locate them by placing an ad in the Hungarian newspaper. No response. A strange coincidence led us to believe that my missing cousin was named Moti (Mordechai) Fleischer. The tip-off came about twenty years ago. I was walking down the street in front of the Supersol on Agron at the corner of King George. The flower vender, named Avie (still there selling flowers,) suddenly called out to me, "Hey are you related to Moti Fleischer in Haifa?" I stopped in my tracks. If this mysterious figure in Haifa had the last name of Fleischer and as the flower vendor repeatedly affirmed, and he looked like me, then this must be my missing cousin. Then we established that a popular rock singer in the 1980s was named Moti Fleischer. Avie claimed that this was the guy he had in mind.

We wanted to believe this was true in order to confirm our self-perception of musical talent in the family. My daughter Rebecca and my son Gabriel both have great musical talent. It must run in the family, even though I am musically incompetent (but I am well above average in my aptitude for the related fields of mathematics and languages). We started doing research on Moti Fleischer. His big hit was called "Absalom, Absalom." Of course we ordered his collected works from the local music store and listened to them but still we did not have a clue how to find him. We tried all the Fleischers in the phone book. No luck. Even when I had been in Santiago some ten years ago I called the two or three Fleischers in the phone book looking for traces. When we were in the North of Israel we traipsed through graveyards looking for clues. All the while we received affirmations that Moti and I looked alike. I was convinced he was the guy.

Then Bracha noticed an article about a wig shop in Miami run by one Jaffa Fleischer. The article commented that she had a husband named Moti who sang at Bar Mitzvahs and other Jewish events. We ran him down living on a suburban street in Bar Harbor. I called Jaffa at the store and finally called Moti at home. To my great disappointment, he was not the guy. He was not connected in any way to Chile or to a Hungarian family. He was born in Lodz like so many talented Jews. He was cordial on the phone and invited us to come but it was clear that he was not my cousin. (When I related this story to Avie, the flower vendor, he did not believe it. He assumed that Moti was just fearful of relatives looking for a handout.)

I think this story tells us more about me than about my family. Why anyone should care so much about these things is beyond me. My cousin Frank did a detailed research on the Lossy family tree a few years ago. His explanation was that it helped him understand his place in history in the face of the dwindling years of his remaining life. I don't think I get that kind of benefit of knowing my blood connections to other people. My sense of it is that it is something like my love of languages. The value of these people is being able to talk to them, to communicate with them now. Dead languages were never of interest to me. Ben Yehuda was the same way. He had to speak Hebrew for it to be relevant to his life.

## *Teaching in Hebrew*

Teaching in a foreign language is the best way to learn it. You have to stand and deliver. You have to face the reality of making mistakes. If you remind yourself that the students make mistakes all the time about the subject matter and yet persevere, you take heart. Mistakes are part of the game.

In my first year in Israel the dean of the law school assigned me to teach two classes – already a gesture of kindness since the norm was to teach four classes. One class was about the law of theft and the other, a seminar about comparative criminal law. The more difficult class was the history of theft because I had to prepare a new series of lectures. I did not realize until now that this is undoubtedly the reason that in 1976 I began my grand opus, *Rethinking Criminal Law*, with the unconventional subject of theft.

In the seminar I had a set of readings, based on cases I had translated into English. It was impossible to teach the class totally in Hebrew because the Hebrew language still lacks the conceptual sophistication of German for discussing the theory of criminal law. I had to teach the class using some German and Russian terminology, which eased my burden in Hebrew.

It was just an accident of history but in those two classes I had two students who went on to become the leading professors of criminal law in Israel. Miri Gur Aryeh signed up for my class on theft. She was quiet during the semester but I decided to give an oral exam in the class (it would have been impossible for me to read their handwriting in Hebrew). She showed up and left a lasting impression of her strong analytic powers and deep knowledge of the subject.

The other student showed up every Tuesday night in a military uniform. He did not speak much either. But he was sufficiently impressed by the course and the method that he decided to learn German in order to continue his studies in Freiburg at the Max Planck Institute. Years later I was walking down the main street of Freiburg with Mota Kremnitzer and we were reminiscing about my time at the university in the early 1970s. I said I thought it was a great seminar. He agreed.

"How do you know?"

"I was the guy in uniform who came every Tuesday night."

At the time he was a military judge working on an advanced degree. Both Miri and Mota have remained close friends. There was another student there at the time and he avoided my classes, a matter which we both find amusing. His name is Meir Dan-Cohen, my friend who would have opted for Hebrew in the Technion. He is a faithful student in his own way, loyal despite his never having received a grade from me.

I cannot quite understand the accidents of history that brought the best students of the younger Israeli generation into my orbit in those years and even a decade later when I met Ron and Karen Shapira at a conference and then invited them to come for a time to New York. I had some attraction but I don't know what it was. I know what attraction to a teacher is because I was overwhelmed by it when I met a great teacher in 1988, overwhelmed despite being close to 50 years old, beyond the age of easy seductions.

### *Meeting Hartman*

The announcement was that David Hartman would give a lecture at the Hillel Foundation at UCLA. I did not know what the event would portend but I had some time on my hands. In order to visit my ailing mother, I traveled often to LA in those days. I usually took a room at the beach near my mother's apartment and rarely did anything except visit her and a few friends.

I remember riding my bike from the beach into Westwood in order to hear Hartman. He swept me off my feet. This is the kind of thing that rarely happens to a grown man, but leaving the lecture and riding home (with my French beret attracting honkers on Wilshire Blvd.), I knew that I had to continue studying, somehow, with Hartman. We corresponded and he invited me to come and study with him.

Hartman's method with potential donors is brilliant. He studies with them privately for a week and then makes a pitch about how valuable the personal experience must have been. He extends the same method to new academic recruits to his institute, even those who did not appear to be potential funders.

I came to Jerusalem and met Hartman in his office. He asked what I had been studying in recent years. Of course, I was doing mostly comparative criminal law but I did not want to say that, so I said I had been studying Immanuel Kant, which was partly true: I gave a seminar at Columbia in Kantian legal and moral thought. Hartman responded, "You fool, don't you know that Kant had no conception of covenant?" He was bringing home an important point about Jewish studies. Most philosophical work since the Enlightenment is based on the principle of universal application. All people are the same. The individual is the relevant unit. Group identities do not count. Thus the right answer at the Technion in the early 20th century – from the universal point of view – would have been to pick German as the language of instruction.

The idea of a covenant between God and Abraham and then later, at Sinai, between God and the entire Jewish people, meant that the Jewish way of thinking was particular, not universal. In fact, in the history of philosophy, particularly in the beginning of the 19th century, there was a controversy between the Kantian universalists and the German and English Romantics who accepted and glorified the particularist perspective. What counts, according to the Romantics, is not reason in the abstract but what we feel, what we the nation feel. The relevant subject is we the collective – not the we consisting of isolated individuals.

I did not know it at the moment, but that conversation with Hartman was the beginning of my life as a conscious Romantic. This became a way of thinking that influenced just about everything I did – from the field of victims' rights to the relevance of war in modern culture. Despite my dubious credentials at the time, Hartman invited me to study with him the following morning.

When I returned some hours later to the same office, Michael Walzer, the famous political philosopher, was already there. He wasn't too pleased to see me because he thought he had Hartman to himself for the week. But we studied together and forged a partnership to promote Jewish philosophical studies in the US. We founded a magazine *S'vara* that ran for about three years. Walzer was very committed to the project. He managed to get several younger members of the institute invited to Princeton for a year and together they produced a series of books and anthologies on Jewish political thought.

Hartman also held a series of conferences for philosophers every summer. These were remarkable events and I felt privileged to be included among some of the great minds in the US. The Hartman method is for small groups to take over the study of a text in both Hebrew and English in the morning (this is called *hevruta*) and then to come together in the afternoon and compare the outcomes of the diverse *hevruta* groups.

In the course of these summer conferences, Suzanne Stone from Cardozo Law School and I became friends. I visited at Cardozo one semester around the year 2000 and we taught a course together based on Walzer's book on Jewish political theory. Then we started teaching the seminar on Biblical Jurisprudence together at Columbia. This was very exciting to me because Suzanne brought expertise in the Bible and I pushed the class to consider jurisprudential issues that were not typically a part of Jewish or religious studies. Our classes consisted mainly of fundamental Protestants and Mormons who know the text cold and came in ready to argue. We could not but succeed. Our class developed a reputation as a "happening." A Christian scholar came from the divinity school next door and a couple of Muslims, in particular my colleague Bernard Freamon, were eager to add their point of view. There was a time when many undergraduate Black students – who knew the Bible very well – joined the class. I felt that I finally found a subject that could reach the student body and take me to a higher level of consciousness as well.

## *Biblical Studies*

My fluency in Hebrew led to a number of discoveries about the Biblical language that go unnoticed among those who read the Bible exclusively in Hebrew or in Hebrew plus one Western language. There is much to learn from the pattern of translation of key concepts into the languages of the world. One of my most significant discoveries was that the concept of *korban*, as sacrifice or victim or offering, as used in the early chapters of Leviticus has a counterpart in the field of criminal law. It turns out that in all the Abrahamic languages (those used in the countries of Judaism, Islam and Christianity) the word for the victim of a crime is the same as the word for the victim of the honorary sacrifice in the Temple. The *korban* is the burnt offering, the victim of the sacrifice as the *korban* is the victim of the crime committed in the secular sphere. The coincidence occurs in Hebrew (*korban*), Turkish (*korban*), German (*Opfer*) Latin languages (*victima*), Russian (*zhertva*), Arabic (*dhiyah*), Hungarian (*áldozat*), Greek (*meri*) – the list goes on and on. It is only in English that there is some ambiguity about the words, sacrifice and victim. But the basic pattern is undeniable. The concept of the victim was transported from the context of Temple sacrifice to the field of secular criminal law. The question is: Why did this happen?

I have pondered possible solutions and described them in various writings in the field. One point is clear to me: The connection has to go deeper than sympathy for the suffering of the sacrificial victim and the victim of a crime. For one thing, sacrificial victimhood carries an element of honor, totally lacking in the case of criminal victims. This element of honor comes through clearly in the debate within Islam about whether the son Abraham is ordered to sacrifice is Isaac or Ishmael. The text says Isaac but Ishmael is the brother who is said to have founded the Islamic branch of the Abrahamic family. Many Muslims insist that the honor of being bound and subject to God's command should go to Ishmael. There may be some honor in falling as a victim in warfare, but not in getting mugged on the street. Yet they are all victims.

To cut to the chase, I will offer you here my explanation of this phenomenon without taking the detour of dismissing all the insufficient explanations. Let me just note that the proper explanation does not lie in the founding moment of Christianity, however tempting this thesis might be. One could say that in the crucifixion, Jesus was punished as a criminal and worshiped as the son of God at the same time. This is true but the connection in the two meanings of *korban* is found in the Jewish tradition and in ancient Greek mythology – both of which must draw on some source other than the Jesus story.

My solution derives from the repeated comments in the early chapters of Leviticus that the sacrificial victim must be without blemish. It must be pure – or in the language of the law, innocent. Here we can see the temptation to use the same word to mark off the innocent victim of crime from the culpable perpetrator. The victim is more than an injured person – he or she is innocent of the wrong that has befallen them. Thus in the world of criminal law, we cherish the innocence of the victim as well as condemn the guilt of the criminal. Our doing this runs against the grain of common knowledge, for we know that in many crimes – domestic homicides, date rapes, shoplifting – the victim is as much involved in the occurrence of the deed as the perpetrator. In the law of torts, we are willing to talk about the comparative fault of the interacting parties, but in criminal law it seems important that we maintain the fiction of evil against good. We cannot divide up the punishment. Perhaps in some cases judges do lower the punishment of the defendant when the victim has been particularly provocative. But the principle of just deserts in punishment resists reduction merely because someone else is also culpable.

Many of my original arguments about the Bible derive from my comparative studies of translations. There is no other way to discover the peculiarities of the *korban* across Abrahamic cultures. If you did not compare translations you would never hit upon another intriguing issue, namely the question: When does

Adam cease being a generic figure (human being) and become a specific person with the name Adam. It is clear that in Genesis 1:26, Adam is a generic being created in the image and likeness of God. And yet in Genesis 1:27 Adam is called "the man," which suggests that there was one of him but still generic. At a certain point, however, Adam must become a proper name. When Genesis 5:3 tells us that Adam lived 130 years and begot a son in his own likeness, he is individualized as is God in the creation of the heavens and the earth. Yet the precise point of transition is subject to controversy.

The translations profile the problem. They begin typically by referring to Adam at the moment of creation as "man" (King James) or as *Menschen* (plural in Luther), but these translators must at a certain point shift to the appellation Adam. Just to take two famous examples, the King James version first uses the word Adam in Genesis 2:19 in the midst of the process of naming the animals: "And out of the ground the Lord God formed every beast of the field, and every fowl of the air; and brought them unto Adam to see what he would call them." Up to this point, Adam is translated as man or the man, but suddenly the reader is expected to know that the man is named Adam.

Luther, by contrast, uses the word *Mensch* to refer to Adam all the way through Chapters One and Two and adopts Adam for the first time in Genesis 3:8, as translated into English: "And they heard the voice of the Lord God walking in the cool of the day and Adam and his wife hid themselves from the presence of the Lord." What explains this difference? These two leading translations assume that they render the text as well as the original Hebrew and their followers think so as well. And yet, behind their translations, there lie unexplained interpretations about the nature of Adam as a generic being or as a specific person.

As between these two options (and there are many more offered by other translations), I think the King James approach has an intuitive appeal. Adam could not be naming animals unless he had a name himself as an individual in communication with

God. But I am sure there are arguments to be offered on behalf of the other translations. The point is that becoming conscious of the problems of translation opens up an entirely new field of inquiry.

This is one of the great intellectual benefits I received from learning Hebrew and making it one of the seven languages in which I have lived my life. I will conclude this chapter by noting as well that the process of learning Hebrew was one of the great intellectual experiences of my life – perhaps because I learned the language so quickly in an atmosphere of great national enthusiasm for the language and the culture.

## Chapter Seven
# My Son: French

I began studying French during my year in Germany, 1964-65. I had decided that if I wanted to make a career in comparative criminal law, I obviously had to learn the supposed language of diplomacy. The best method at the time seemed to be the Berlitz Institute and there was one conveniently located in downtown Freiburg. I was curious to know how Berlitz became so successful teaching languages by total immersion. I went to a few lessons but was quickly disappointed. In the second or third lesson, the teacher started drilling me on the names of flowers in French. I thought this was absurd. I barely know the names of the flowers in English. It is of no practical value to learn trivia of this sort at the outset of a course. The best method, I was convinced, was the Army method used in my Russian course at Cornell: Learn the sentences that you need to know to negotiate critical functions when you are shot down behind enemy lines. Sorry, Berlitz, you did not pass the test.

As a next step, I went to an intensive course offered in the city of Tour on the Loire River slightly south of Paris. Susan and our daughter Deborah, then about six months old, came with me, and we found a pension where we could have home-cooked meals at midday. A few other boarders working on their French joined us at the table. The landlady sat with us to encourage conversation in French. I remember one curious aristocratic type who claimed that he would establish his career over lunch – between the appetizer and *piece de resistance*. Perhaps he has.

The remarkable event of our one month stay in Tour is that we sought out the Jewish community. This was going to be the season of Passover, the first Passover that I had taken seriously, and therefore we were open to an invitation to attend a *seder* with the local rabbi. Much to our surprise, he did indeed invite us to join him. Thus we had our first *seder* circa 1965 – in French, with some key passages in Hebrew – in a large room next to the synagogue, in the charming city of Tour. I made a point of abstaining from bread for the entire week, the first time in my life.

My days were spent in the language course at the university. There I had an experience that reminded me of the third grade in Glendale. I was put in the same class with German students learning the basics of the tongue on the other side of the Rhein. We spoke the same language. Then the teacher asked me to write something on the board. I wrote in the style I had learned in Glendale when I was seven years old. Everyone in the class understood immediately that I was not German. They learn a distinctive form of handwriting, which is apparently much different from the style taught in the United States. I could sense this when I compared my father's Hungarian-educated cursive writing with my own. My accent and my command of German did not "out" me but my doing what I learned in the third grade most certainly did.

I wish this had remained my sole memory of Tour. Unfortunately, I returned once on a Friday evening circa 1980 with my younger daughter Rebecca. It was the end of a long cycling trip in the Loire Valley and we were exhausted. There was a convention in town – of lawn bowlers, I think – and all the rooms seemed to be taken. No problem, I told her, let's go to the synagogue and I am sure someone will put us up. We went to the service after a quick change in a bathroom someplace and afterwards we started asking around. It was a different rabbi and apparently "there arose a king who knew not Joseph." No one was interested in helping us out. It was dark and we could not ride further. The only option was to find a cab, put our bikes in the trunk, and ride to Fountainebleau, the next town over in the valley. There we found a room.

## *Cycling in France*

The cycling trip with Rebecca was one of many pleasurable cycling trips I have taken, beginning in 1970. I got the idea from a fun-loving colleague at UCLA named Joel Rabinowitz. I took my first trip alone and learned, rather awkwardly, how to do this in a sensible way. I flew from LA to London, bought my bicycle and panniers there, and then took the bicycle, by ferry, to one of the northern ports (after that unnecessary import of an English bicycle, I started buying Peugots in Paris). Since I had been in Tour once before, I proceeded by train to the Loire Valley. The geography of the region and the clues it offered to the language fascinated me. I discovered that there were in fact two rivers and two valleys. La vallee du Loir and Le val de la Loire, the former being the significant river, more widely known.

After my first trip in 1970, I would return often, sometimes alone, sometimes with a companion, to spend several weeks cycling, mostly in the Loire Valley but also along the Dordogne and a place that I loved, but was far to the south: Les gorges du Tarn.

France is a cyclist's paradise because the French road system is a thick grid of small country roads as well as *routes nationales* that move traffic at much higher speeds. On the country roads, marked in white on the map, you can ride for hours encountering few cars. These trips – more solitary traveling than I have done anywhere else – were the framework for my learning French.

I recall telling Gerry Goldfarb before the trip that I would take a chess set with me and set it up in bars, hoping that passersby would want to play a game or two. He thought this was very funny. He did not think Frenchmen would even notice me, not to mention sit down and play chess with me. He was both right and wrong. In my bars the locals were happy to talk to me, but a spontaneous game of chess was too much to expect.

In the course of the last 30 years I have made cycling trips at least 15 times in France, each trip was about two to three weeks. That is a lot of time to be spending on the bicycle, but it served very well to keep me in good shape and of course, my French got better with every ride. The language study was enhanced by reading Le Monde every day, usually in the morning with croissants and coffee, a delightful ritual.

The route of Tour to Anger in the Loire Valley is one of my favorite rides. I know the possible overnight stops along the way almost by heart, even though the available B&Bs seem to change every few years. I usually roll into Anger and stay in a hotel in the center square. It is nothing special but I guess I am a creature of habit. After a shower and a rest, I would usually go to the one art house in town – *Quatre Sons Coups* – that plays films in *version originale* – V.O. – in the original language. The Loire Valley has remained relatively free of traffic because the heavy long-distance traffic gravitates to the turnpikes intelligently positioned on two hills overlooking the sides of the valley.

Lately, I have discovered the bliss of cycling along the Atlantic Coast, which Bracha and I did in the summers of 2007 and 2010. We found magnificent hotels along the water, fronting the cliffs, not less glamorous than those in Carmel, California. Indeed the Western Atlantic Coast is much like the Western Pacific Coast, except that the summer sun stays high in the sky until about 9:30 p.m. Of course, the food is delicious in France, even though perhaps a little less varied than in New York. One thing about the French culture that the tourist must adjust to is that a trip in this integrated part of Europe is a throwback to the times of a nationally zealous culture. Though once in a while service people speak English, everything surrounding you – newspapers, television, road signs, advertisement, cinema and TV programs (all dubbed) – everything is hermetically sealed in French. No other language is taken seriously. The trend seems to be towards more isolation, particularly in the countryside. This is the opposite of Jerusalem, where at least five languages are heard on a regular basis and broadcast on TV, infiltrating daily life.

*The Scientologists*

I do not recall how it happened but in 1977 I was called in to observe a trial in Paris of the Scientologists charged with allegations of fraud. Someone put together an international team of observers to watch what went on in the courtroom and to be prepared to generate publicity against the French legal system if things went awry. This was something like our project in the Soviet Union, which we tried out some five years before. My assumption was that the same could work in every country as a way of keeping courts honest in politically sensitive trials.

I do not have much sympathy with the Scientology mumbo jumbo about getting "clear" – a spiritual state supposedly measured by a device they call the E-meter. The founder, L. Ron Hubbard (1911-1986) was a clever, though controversial, huckster. I recall he lived on a boat offshore in order to avoid being personally sued for his marketing Scientology. Yet I see no harm in their advertising miracle cures for people who want to part with their money.

So far as I know, American prosecutors have left the Scientologists alone. There has not even been a private lawsuit by a disgruntled "unclear person" to get his money back. The position of the group in Europe has been much more controversial.

The British and French have often alleged that the group thrives on criminal fraud, but in fact the fraud is no more egregious than the marketing of most vitamin pills. They sell various items by mail order and make a few dollars. I found the French zeal to convict the representatives of the "church" inexplicable.

I think that our international observation team had some impact. The judge took us seriously. However, our intervention hardly ended the problems of the Scientologists in the French courts. Even today the trials continue and the issues are basically the same. Are they are entitled to practice as a religion? Do they use fraud to secure contributions from the faithful?

The best part of my 1977 trip to Paris is that it took place during a semester I was visiting at Yale. Part of my negotiated fee was the right to take the Supersonic Transport, the SST flown by Air France and British Air, back from Paris in order to make my class the next day. This was an experience I now cherish because the SST has since gone out of business. International businessmen no longer know what it is like to have lunch in Paris and be home in plenty of time for dinner. The only problem with the plane was the unbearable noise to the people below the cracking of the sound barrier. In the plane we felt nothing. We, the passengers, savored the gauges that reported the ground speeds as variations of Mach 1. The noise led to the prohibition of the plane in the New York area. I had to fly into Washington and then ironically take a slow prop flight to an airport close to New Haven. Whether I helped the Scientologists or not, they were good to me.

It is doubtful whether my professional life in France could ever reach a much higher plateau than in this case. I certainly made an effort to establish a relationship with the leading French scholar of criminal law, Mireille Delmas-Marty. I looked her up for coffee in Paris, invited her to come and give a lecture at Columbia, and appeared with her in numerous international conferences. Once I had a semester in residence at Reid Hall, which was the Columbia pied-a-terre in France. I had a little office and exchanged ideas with the students and faculty in residence. Not much turned on criminal law. When Mireille spoke about criminal law, her performance was a work of art. She spoke in high abstractions and virtually nobody could follow the argument. There was another American there at the time, Dianne Amman, who has done some work on the basis of her collaboration with Mireille.

It is generally known that France does not participate in the debate about the theory of criminal law that dominates the field in

Germany, Italy, Spain, and Latin America. One reason for this is that French criminal law is considered a form of private rather than public law. Those who become criminal lawyers must compete with all the business and commercial and corporate lawyers in the national aggregation – the competitive exam for university posts. With all the financial rewards in the other fields, it is surprising that French scholars opt for criminal law at all.

No one else in the world would say that criminal law should be classified as private law, so why do the French say this? The most my associate, Mathilde Cohen, and I have been able to figure out is that private law is about the scope of rights and duties, while public law regulates the spheres of governmental autonomy, as typified by administrative agencies. The characteristic of the public sphere is that this is where the state and its offices exercise discretion, free from the tight restraint of rules. Its purpose is to promote the proper proportionality between means and ends in the exercise of governmental power. Since criminal law is a matter of rights that cabin the state's power to impose duties of compliance, it makes sense to think of criminal law – like private law – as a body of strict enforcement.

It is tempting but not correct to think of criminal law as the general field of equal enforcement – all offenders should be treated equally, with due regard for their personal culpability. Yet, at the procedural level, prosecutors obviously have special access to the powers implied in the system of law enforcement.

Admittedly, the French theory of private law is a bit of an outlier in European legal theory. So far as I know, the same theory has not appealed to other legal systems in Europe. The irony of France's exceptional but rigorous view is that the French lawyers would surely know that criminal law is treated as private law (they have to take their exam in criminal law along with the other private law subjects) but they have not offered a theory about why this is so.

My study of languages has led to many experiences that would have not come the way of an ordinary law professor. As much as the joy I received from my wandering life, I also exposed myself to some separation and alienation, the risk of which lies latent in a life already divided by linguistic loyalties. Falling in love with someone from another culture is a dangerous gamble. She might leave and return to a home where you have few chances of survival – professionally and financially. Even worse, she might leave and take your child with her.

I am not surprised that in the mid-1980s, I fell in love with Muriel (Michal in Hebrew) Hollander, a woman who was fluent in Hebrew and French as well as perfectly competent in English. After living together for a short time she announced that she was about five months pregnant and returning immediately to Belgium where her parents lived. She was Jewish and would undoubtedly want a circumcision for a male child. I was clearly the passive party in the entire transaction. I ended up present at Gabriel's birth and had the honor of participating in the ceremony of the *briss*.

On the surface of things, everyone was very cordial. We agreed on his first two names, Gabriel Dan, the latter name in honor of Michal's recently deceased brother. But the signs of irreconcilable tension were evident in our failure to agree on the family name. She insisted on her family name Hollander on the birth certificate, though she did add Fletcher as an additional forename, and I did virtually the opposite by registering him as an American citizen under the name Gabriel Dan Hollander Fletcher.

When he was old enough to appreciate the mild insanity of this arrangement, he had lots of fun mocking his name by jumbling the order of his four names.

It became clear rather rapidly that Michal had no intention of returning to the US or of living with me under any circumstances. She refused to allow me to spend time with Gabriel alone. This state of affairs began a prolonged series of court battles about visitation rights. In the beginning Michal did not seem to care about financial support. She would have been happy to go it alone – with no sharing of parental rights and no support payments.

*Gabriel and George in Brussels.*

This led to innumerable audiences in the *Palais de Justice* in Brussels and files upon files of pleadings and court judgments on my visitation rights, coupled with rulings about child support. Once Michal realized that she could not be the exclusive parent, of course she wanted to receive as much as she could get.

The process of going to Brussels, appearing in court, arguing my case, sometimes with a lawyer, sometimes without, proved to be just another interesting episode in my collection of international cases. I could not but appreciate the educational advantage of learning how the Belgian system works and improving my French. The legal issues were not taxing. It was basically a matter of arguing that as Gabriel was getting older he should spend more time with his father. Eventually, when he turned five or six, I gained the right to take him on long vacations, two or three weeks at a time, and we had a ball devoting this time to hiking and cycling treks in Europe, usually with groups of other travelers. We hiked the Dolomites, rode our bicycles across the Loire Valley, and trekked around the peninsula of Cornwall. All of these and many more of the same genre worked out fairly well, largely because I had the time and money to treat my son to adventures that most kids could only dream about.

Of course, Hollander made things as difficult as possible. Every time Gabriel came she put him through a humiliating ritual of counting all of his pieces of clothes on the doorstep before he was allowed to enter. She took the toys I gave him and stored them in a special place in the basement, to be retrieved only when I was there. She sometimes refused to meet the court's time schedule, which was a form of abusive conduct the court would examine. In order to secure her compliance I repeatedly asked the court to fine her if she failed to comply. This move produced the only humorous line of the trials. Michal's lawyer – a very clever and determined advocate named Hiernaux – tried to satirize my requests with the line, "*Ah, Monsieuer Fletcher est un professeur de droit pénal. He aime punir.*" (Fletcher is a professor of criminal law. He loves to punish.") *Chapeau! Hiernaux.*

I have no regrets about investing all this time and money in an effort to be a good father to Gabriel, but it did not really work out as I expected. Whatever the subtle propaganda at home was I could not combat it by showing Gabriel a good time from time to time. He was never afraid of me and only rarely hostile or rebellious. Yet there was something missing. It did not matter that he called me "papa." In his soul I never became his papa. Gabriel came to New York to visit a couple of times and spent a considerable time with my daughters Deborah and Rebecca but they never bonded in a way that could sustain their relationship over time and distance. When he turned thirteen and celebrated his bar mitzvah at the Main Synagogue in Brussels (brilliantly, by the way), Deborah made a special trip from Los Angeles to be there. Cousins Karen and David joined me as well. We have fond memories of this and all the other trips but the resulting emotional bond to Gabriel probably exists more in our minds than in his.

My misfortune with Gabriel stands in contrast to a relationship I had with a boy the same age, Mihaly Lupas, whom I called Mickey. Mickey moved into my apartment with his mother Daniela Lupas sometime in the 90s, when he was about four years old. He immediately went for the front closet and converted it into a vertical bedroom. He slept on the shelves and climbed back and forth on a series of rope ladders he constructed. All of these kids were the same age, within six weeks of birth – Mickey, Gabriel, and my granddaughter Rachel. Often, in the summers, we were all together at the same time. Also, there were memorable twosomes. Rachel and Mickey spent a month once at the beach in Normandy. Rachel loved to join Mickey in his vertical lair. Gabriel kept more to himself but thought of Mickey more or less as a brother. Alas, these ties seem to have weakened over the years. I almost succeeded in creating an environment that enriched all of their lives. Perhaps, in the long run, it will.

I am left with two thoughts about children, which have run, often coursed, through my mind. The first is the advice my mother gave me: "Do not live for your children, Georgie." This was a form of emancipation because she was telling me, in effect, that I was free to live my life without worrying about her needs. The other is a little piece of wisdom I made up and fits perfectly in the context of this book. Children are languages. If you do not pay attention to them, they will abandon you. Glory be to the reader who can reconcile these attitudes in one consistent approach toward children. You have to pay them enough attention so that they stay yours, but not too much that you and they become dependent on each other.

Chapter Eight

# My Calling: English

My education from kindergarten through graduate work in law was mostly in English. One year was in German and the other languages occupied me, as I have detailed, a good part of the time. But the bedrock of my understanding of the world was communicated to me in the English language. This should mean that I have an affection for the language and that its supposedly empirical influence on English philosophy has the same impact on me. None of this is true. English is for me like a nest for a bird, to alight, from time and time, before it wings forth to unknown domains.

I probably picked up this disdain for education in English from my father. Not only did he hate the language, but he thought the school systems in Beverly Hills and Hollywood atrocious. His prejudice was based mainly on the light treatment of European history (which is true) and the virtual disregard for the study of languages – obviously true.

I had very little experience writing, though picking up the grammar of English was, in my mind, child's play. In fact I am so committed to the grammar they then taught in school that I am constantly irritated by the younger generation's inability to speak correctly. This is obvious in the media, where it is common for characters to say something like "I wish I was in Hawaii." or "If I was in Hawaii right now I would dive into ocean." These uses of the subjunctive form of "was" are obviously false. In both cases the correct verb is "were." But 10 will get you 1 that you do not hear the correct form of speech on television anymore – or in politics – or even in educational settings. Something happened to fifth grade grammar. The aliens must have erased it from our consciousness.

Another bête noire of mine is the correct "different from" rather than the more common spoken form "different than." The reason for this mistake is fairly simple. In the minds of native speakers, "different" is assimilated to other adjectives of comparison – like pretty, tall, short, or long. All of these take "than" in the comparative form – prettier than, taller than, shorter than, and longer than. By analogy, one should say "different than." The problem is that unlike the others, difference is not a matter of degree. Something is either different from something else or not. You don't have the forms "more" and "less" different, at least not in correct communicative speech. Also, the base of "different" is the verb to differ. As a verb, differ already defines a categorical difference, not one of degree. You either differ or you don't. Perhaps this is more than the reasonable reader would want to know about these matters, but since I have an attachment to this explanation, I take the liberty of sharing it with you. I locate myself in the spirit of Arthur Lagawier, my idiosyncratic teacher of Hebrew: Little known but correct theories should be shouted from the rooftops.

Grammar – even with its ill-defined contours – was like easy math and therefore I mastered it with a vengeance. Reading was harder and, despite my parents' complaints, I rarely read a book. I did enjoy Shakespeare when we read some of the plays in class. The main attraction for me was memorizing the key soliloquies and delivering them in class. It was the presentation of self, more than the literature, that interested me. The consequence of my poor reading habits in my early years was that I found myself at the age of 16 with a vocabulary unsuitable for admission to a first-rate university. I scored a perfect 800 on the math section of the SATs, but my English score put me in the 60th percentile. In order to make up for this performance I had to master all the books on English grammar and vocabulary I could find. I read Fowler's *Modern English Usage* from cover to cover.

In my early years the only subject in which I excelled was arithmetic and then math. I had no sense of being smarter than the others in my class until my teacher in the fourth grade at Horace Mann School in Beverly Hills asked us to do sums on the board. It became clear fairly soon that I was much faster and more accurate than the other kids. Steve Gluckman was my major competition. This little bit of recognition sustained my self-confidence, at least until I hit ninth grade at Beverly Hills High School.

The intellectual demands of high school were not higher, but they were more complex. The curriculum was impossible to master in its entirety. You had to make choices. We spoke then of "solids" and "electives." There were only six periods, and gym was required. You could not consistently take five solids because there were other requirements, such as art and music and even, believe it or not, drivers' education, it being assumed that every reasonable person would want to drive at the age of 16. I had the good fortune of signing up for Mechanical Drawing. I don't remember whether it counted as a solid or not, but it did not matter. I fell totally in love with drawing by T-square, reasoning through perspectives, and inking my drawings. For me this was real work and I was very proud of my productions. I did a three-dimensional drawing of a gear that made me feel like a professional.

Beverly High had the best architecture-preparation program imaginable. Many of the students in that first year – including Steve Gluckman, I believe – went on to become noteworthy architects in Los Angeles. This Camelot I took for granted came to an unwitting end when the family moved to Hollywood for financial reasons and I chose to transfer to Hollywood High, which was much closer. This was the worst decision I ever made. I just assumed that the things I loved at Beverly – like German and Mechanical Drawing – would be replicated in the LA school system.

The difference in the student culture between the two schools was astonishing. The elite at Beverly were the smart kids with professional futures. Among them were a few musicians and offspring of movie producers. The dominant group at Hollywood could not have been more obviously different. They were the toughs who picked particular benches as their own and established their prestige by deciding who could sit with them and not. It was something like a prison yard hierarchy, based on football and prowess in hand-to-hand combat.

Nonetheless I was able to find the few college-bound Jewish kids at Hollywood High, and actually they were more interesting people than my cohort at Beverly High. One (Mike Shapiro) spoke fluent Russian (though I did not know it until later). One later quit Harvard to roam the world – something I would never dare do. He came back, settled down, finished school, married his high school sweetheart, and then tired of being a lawyer, eventually became a Protestant Minister (Brad Bunnin). Another became a famous TV announcer during the O.J. trial (Roger Cossack). Another spoke fluent Yiddish and became a successful dentist in Beverly Hills (Simon Gamer). We were all social outcasts in high school but with rich lives ahead of us.

There was a period in the eleventh grade when I was obviously depressed and my studies were unproductive. My parents seriously explored the possibility of sending me to school in Switzerland. They were right to consider the option but I guess they didn't have the savvy to pull it off. My depression continued until I discovered my abilities in debate and public discourse. My speech teacher, Jack Bell, recognized my talents and took an interest in me the way no other teacher had. Also because of the Hollywood allure, the girls in acting class were more attractive and, on the whole, even smarter. They had an air of sophistication that high schools girls in Los Angeles generally lacked. I found myself obsessed with one or another of them for over a year, and oddly, the aspiring actresses were reciprocally attracted to me.

Andrea Sheridan (later Ordin), who went on to become

an important lawyer in LA and was recently appointed the first female county counsel, said she fell in love with me after hearing me recite the Gettysburg Address to the entire student body. I cherish this moment, though I knew it was a fleeting sentiment (and hopefully no embarrassment to her career). I wished I had the same attraction for other women. I knew, however, that I did not – not even for Andrea, who forgot about Gettysburg a few days later.

## *College Years*

Going to Cornell did very little to raise my self-esteem with women. The male/female ratio on campus was about 3 to 1, and I did not seem to be in the lucky one third. We used to go out scouring the local girls' colleges in the Finger Lake District, but in my first few years I never seemed to connect to the Eastern girls. I did my best – next to bribing the coach to put me on the football team – to make myself attractive to the opposite sex. I ran for class president and quite surprisingly – with the help of my newly-made friend Gerry Goldfarb – won the race. This was less cool than I thought it would be. Student politics took up a lot of time, with little payoff. It was, alas, not the college equivalent of being on the football team.

My second year was almost a total waste. I lived in the ZBT fraternity house, which had a fabulous cliff-side location, but was hardly the place to expect to study. There were three of us in a small suite. I was lucky to get any sleep, not to mention a chance to think or read or write in private. In those days, quite amazingly, fraternities were segregated, of course, by gender and almost 100% by race and religion. We were a Jewish house. Of course, there was almost nothing Jewish about it. No kosher meals. No celebration of the holidays. The most Jewish aspect was trying to set up joint events with the *shiksa* (gentile) sororities. My friend Goldfarb ended up in a lower status Jewish house but this had little impact on our friendship. (How perverse that I should be proud of that!)

The fraternity system was the college equivalent of the bench rankings at Hollywood High. I thought I did my part for truth and justice by "adopting" a visiting Japanese student I met at a conference and getting him some kind of associate status at the House. He later moved into the Telluride House, which was much better, finished his studies at Columbia, and went on to become an important diplomat. About ten years later, Tatsuro Kanugi was the UN representative in Jerusalem living in the Arab part of town. For some reason he had difficulties coming over to visit me in the Western part where our apartment was located, but he finally came. Now it was his turn to "adopt" a Jew.

The one good thing about Cornell was that there was a strong independent movement made of pre-hippy intellectuals who lived mostly in Collegetown flats next to campus. The several novels written about life at Cornell gravitate toward the intrigues of the Collegetown apartments.

However miserable the second year might have been, the end of the year culminated in one of the most dramatic encounters of my life, one that continues to influence my legal sensibilities. In May of 1958, at the end of my year, we experienced what I think was the harbinger of the Berkeley and Columbia riots of the 1960s. The background to these riots is important because I fear the social conditions at the time have been forgotten. In the 1950s, the university thought of itself as acting "in loco parentis" with the right and duty to impose sexual restraints on the lives of the students. Boys and girls lived in separate dorms. Boys could move out to apartments, as I did, but girls were bound to the dormitory system for four years. Further, they had to be in their rooms by certain hours and they could not have boys in their rooms. The university even tried to regulate sexual contact in apartments off campus. I believe there was a rule that held that even if a boy and a girl were in a room in Collegetown, the door to their room had to be open at least three inches. I think these were called "parietal" rules but the term is rarely in use now.

This was a pre-revolutionary situation. No one complained

very much about the parietal rules. If the right organizers came along to make us conscious of the discrimination and the slightly salacious intrusion into our lives, however, the system was bound to burst.

In May 1958, there happened to be some extraordinary radical leaders on campus. Cornell was the home to a strong literary tradition beginning with E.B. White in the early part of the century and then Kurt Vonnegut – an editor of the Cornell Daily Sun in his last years of college before being called off to the war in Europe. At the time, the literary stars were Thomas Pynchon, later author of *Mason-Dixon* and other leading novels, and Richard Fariña, actor and chic personality, who soon after his Cornell years wrote *Been Down so Long it Looks Up to Me*. Even without Nabokov there was enough star power in the English building to give us a sense that life was lived and recorded more intensely in Ithaca than any other college town.

Fariña was a mysterious character. He was just a few years older, but because he was away in military service for that time, he acted as though he had two decades more of experiences on the frontlines. His father was Cuban and his mother Irish, so the rumors were that in his absence from campus, he was fighting both for the IRA and Castro in Cuba. In fact, I think he was in the US Navy. In the late 1950s, any elaboration was acceptable if it made a good story.

Fariña was the de facto leader of the growing protest movement against the parietal rules. He drew J. Kirk Sale, then editor of the *Cornell Daily Sun*, into his orbit. Sale was an aristocratic figure, and went along probably because it seemed the noble thing to do. In late May, the protest spilled over into a student march to President Malott's house and once there, the angry students started throwing eggs and reportedly, more dangerous objects, perhaps even a small explosive. There were no serious injuries, but the *New York Times* reported on May 24 that a Cornell dean was hit during the egg-throwing. Fariña and Sale were apparently there, but for some reason Pynchon wasn't.

The University Administration did not call in the police; according to their understanding, found in many town and gown relationships, the administration would try to solve the problem with their local disciplinary boards. This is where I came into the story. The standard pattern for a student politico at Cornell after the second year was either to shoot for higher office (presidency or vice presidency of the school) or to join the Men's Judiciary Board. I don't remember how I was selected but because I had been in the upper echelons of the class government, the choice was pro forma.

My first case, as I recall, was the disciplinary action against Fariña and Sale. The hearing gave me my first education in due process and its pathologies. The defendants had lawyers but the Board ruled that the lawyers could not speak for their clients. There were similar deviations from our common understanding of a fair trial but the most disturbing to an untutored legal mind like mine was the associate dean's reading letters from the alumni about the necessity of imposing harsh sanctions. I did not know about the concept of hearsay at the time, but I knew that I was the judge in the case and therefore no one from the outside should be dictating the results (recall the reaction of Judge Stern to the State Department's lawyer in the German hijacking case). The decision finally came down to whether we would vote for an official or unofficial sanction, the former appearing on the transcript and the latter, not. This was very similar to the problem faced in the Végvári case. We were up all night deliberating on the case. Mine was the swing vote and I am not sure how I finally voted, but I fear that I caved in, in favor of the official sanction. The headline of the Daily Sun on May 29 read:

"MJB Paroles Fariña, Sale on Riot Charge."

This headline is doubly amusing. First, there was so little due process that I am afraid there was no "riot charge." If the administrators had the name of a crime in mind, it was probably something like "conduct unbecoming a student." Also, the use of the word "parole" is a tickle. They were not in confinement, and certainly not in jail. There was nothing conditional about the sanction as there is about parole. The Daily Sun took all of this to be high drama, which of course it was for us as well. More accurately, in another article, the Sun reported that 36 women were reprimanded – presumably by their own judiciary board – for intentionally violating the rules on closing hours.

I learned more from this experience than any law school course could teach me. No one ever had to lecture me again about the need to observe the rules of due process, however strongly the "alumni" and their equivalents clamor for blood.

I was relieved the following year to get out of student government and devote myself to my studies. It was becoming clear to me that however ill educated I was in the humanities, I was more interested in law and philosophy than in math and physics – the test scores be damned. A group of friends from ZBT plus a couple of other guys, independents, and I took a three-bedroom apartment for six in downtown Ithaca. I found a corner of the attic that I could convert into a private study and for the first time in my college life I found a place where I could be alone and think. I was studying philosophy with Norman Malcolm then and I devoted myself, mind and soul, to writing papers for him. He often quoted Wittgenstein that philosophy was not the history of philosophy. This was a liberating message designed to get us to undertake the required original thinking. The paper topics were on questions you never heard of before, e.g. "Can two people feel the same pain?" For the first time, sitting alone in that attic, working all night on papers for Malcolm, I felt that I was becoming an intellectual.

I also studied international law that year with Herbert Briggs, the author of the casebook we used. For his time he was a major figure in the field. He was not a lawyer, which was perhaps good for an introduction to non-lawyers. Nonetheless, I learned something about how to use the law library and found myself comfortable in reading and analyzing the cases. Law school began to seem inevitable.

Living in Ithaca was a romantic experience in more ways that one. I walked back and forth to campus along the spectacular gorges that connect the campus with the town. I enjoyed my new life as a loner dedicated to my studies. Then suddenly, women became accessible. I met a girl from Ithaca College who drove me batty when we could (or could not) get our hands on each other. She was probably quite intelligent, but I never had a chance to calm down and focus on her intellectual charms.

The big event of the year was my meeting a super-intelligent dropout from Cornell who continued to live on the hill descending into town from campus. She became my tutor in all matters of the mind and the flesh. Since I was working so hard on my writing, she helped me edit my papers. She seemed a little crazy but I found her questions about the contradictions of life very charming. They fit perfectly into my vision of myself as a budding intellectual. She had some writing tics which I continue to cherish, one of them was never to use the word "such." It is true that most writers of academic English vastly overuse the word. I avoid it as a gesture of piety. And I feel squeamish when I notice my colleagues slipping into this typical academic distortion of good writing.

Looking back on that year living in Ithaca, cut off from all the relationships that held me back for two years, searching out real people who lived on a schedule and in a style they packaged themselves, I felt that I was coming alive – not only as an intellectual but as a young man.

At the end of my third year, we had a major family crisis. My father was sick and the family informed me that they could not afford to send me back for the fourth year. I had originally gotten a fellowship but it was based on need and therefore the stipend was low. Perhaps I could have figured out some way to get financial aid, but frankly I was exhausted by these intense experiences at Cornell and I was relieved by the thought of returning to California.

The family plan was that I would enroll in the University of California in Berkeley. The tuition was cheap for California residents and I could still be an hour or so from home. Upon arriving in Berkeley – after an all night train ride from LA – I looked for a way of life that would be as far as possible from my socially entrenched existence at Cornell. For some reason, my cousin Paul  was also transferring from the University of Chicago to Berkeley. So we decided to live in adjacent rooms in a rooming house. That lasted a few days. Paul got fed up with school and dropped out. He went across the Bay and took up rooming with hippies in Haight-Ashberry or nearby. I had no desire whatsoever to join him. It seemed much too freaky for me. But I did not know what to do. Fairly soon I found myself uncomfortable in that rooming house and found an isolated room at the end of a long garden path near the Rose Garden on the 1400 block of Euclid Avenue. I fell in love with the garden, the solitude, and the life that I created with books and fresh air around me. There was a single bed in the corner of the secret chamber but as befitting a hermit's room it remained, as far as I recall, as chaste as a monk's cot.

My only problem was that I could not study philosophy as much as I wanted to. The only way to finish in one year was to major in math and that meant taking two math courses a semester, a burden, but one that I easily bore in terms of mental energy and time. My libido yearned for philosophy. Fortunately I had John Searle, fresh back from Oxford, as passionate as a young man in love. With residues of my memory of Malcolm, Searle became the model of the intellectual I wanted to be.

One good thing about that year of solitude is that I could enjoy a good meal with good company once in a while with my cousins Frank and Rella Berk Lossy (the second Rella named directly after the deceased heroine). They lived about a mile further up Euclid and off a few streets. Sometimes they also invited Paul, who was seemingly grateful to get away from his hippie environs and enjoy a home-cooked meal. Once they invited us over at the same time and we presented versions of ourselves that flouted the family rumors.

When we were about 14 years old (and there are only six weeks between our birthdays) Paul was the serious student with an impressive bar mitzvah and perfect grades behind him. I was rebellious, spoiled, irreverent about Judaism and generally intolerable. I think family difficulties accounted for my eccentric behavior. As a result of coercion imposed by Uncle Géza in Buenos Aires, my father had to pay some alleged debt based on their war-time trading in leather goods. I have no idea whether it was a valid debt or extortion on the part of Géza. In any event we suddenly found ourselves broke. My parents opened a cleaning store to make ends meet. We moved from our spacious suburban Beverly Hills home and had to crouch into two rooms above the cleaning store. I was still in Beverly High and full of shame that my friends' parents had to drop me off in front of the cleaning store, or even a block away in order to conceal my address. We shared a staircase with the unit next door where the occupant was drunk all the time and scared me out of my skin. If I hadn't become obnoxious, I would have probably taken to narcotics (had they been available) to ease the pain.

In any event, by the age of 20, the situation had reversed itself. Paul was the hippy in training – rebellious, impolite, and incapable of settling down in a program of study. I was orderly and gentlemanly, thrilled by my newfound solitude at the end of the garden path. We were invited, presumably for the first time together, to Frank's and Rella's for dinner. The great moment occurred when the two crossed paths in the kitchen and one asked the other, "So which one of these is supposed to be the obnoxious cousin?"

Since that time Paul has lost most of his hippy rebelliousness and in fact now lives much in the way I did at the end of the garden path on Euclid. He enjoys solitude, accompanied by his lovely wife Susan, on the top of one of the canyons on the West Side of LA.

In February of 1960, the year I was living on the rose garden path, my father died. The phone call is burned in my memory.

I immediately flew down to LA and did what I could to comfort my mother. These were very difficult times for her and for me. My sister's marriage was in trouble, which meant that she moved back and forth, with her daughter Cheryl, from Philadelphia to the Park La Brea in Los Angeles. Lillian was also sick with lupus and in and out of City of Hope. There was need for comfort and support all around. I was probably of most aide to Cheryl until her mother died in 1962 and her father took her back with him to live in Philadelphia.

My studies were a good reason to return to my rose garden in Berkeley. As I was returning and walking down the path, I saw my landlords working in their garden – hoeing, planting, preparing for spring. I sensed a renewal of nature, the cycle of life. This gave me great comfort in thinking about my father's death. My mother came up to visit shortly thereafter and she enjoyed herself enormously to see where I lived and to savor the beauty of my environs.

By the end of the year I was ready to take off into the world again. I wrote about fifty letters to English-speaking schools around the world inquiring whether they needed a math teacher. I got a fascinating collection of replies, with several offers. Costa Rica, Turkey, and other places offered me jobs on the spot. Israel was interested but they said I had to teach in Hebrew. Little did I know then that I could have learned the requisite Hebrew in two or three months. Roberts College in Istanbul was the most tempting offer. They asked for a three-year commitment. I had visions of teaching there and then traveling around Europe every summer and learning all the languages I could. (Later I learned that Orhan Pamuk, one my favorite writers, studied there.)

But then I got scared about the draft. The rule at the time was that if you stayed in school you could maintain your exemption. The thought of spending two or three years in the army terrified me. I did not want to take the chance of testing my fundamental hostility toward authority – not to mention the boredom of hanging around the barracks.

There was a time, however, that I was intrigued by learning a language from the impressive military language school in Monterrey. I walked into a recruiting office someplace in California and told the recruiting officer that I would sign if he would send me to Monterrey. Alas, he said: Sign up first and then we'll talk. I had to pass on that one.

In the end, I decided to stay close to my mother and attend the first year of law school at UCLA. I actually enjoyed living with her in the same apartment we shared with my father when I was in high school. Just about the time I arrived home at the Park La Brea, my mother asked me to join her at a reception she did not want to attend alone. By accident I met a young woman there whose family was part of our Hungarian-Jewish crowd. She was a senior in English lit at USC. She was a cousin to Paul and related therefore indirectly to me. Susan and I started dating immediately. She was an interesting conversational partner, attractive, but hardly a swinger. She kept the reigns on sexually but since I had so little experience myself I hardly noticed.

The real consequence of my not running off to Turkey and taking the risk of getting drafted is that I got inveigled by another kind of commitment. After a year and a half of dating and a few kisses, Susan and I got engaged to marry in the summer of 1962. In the meantime, she graduated with honors, got a prestigious Wilson fellowship (Paul eventually got the same honor), and made plans to go to graduate school at Columbia.

I was weighed down by the first year of law school at UCLA. It was both exhilarating and painful. Some of my teachers were superb – Bill Cohen in torts, Murray Schwartz in criminal law, James Chadbourne in civil procedure. The best of all was the philosopher Herbert Morris, who was not formally assigned to be my teacher, but sought me out after Murray Schwartz told him that a student in the class had an uncanny grasp of theoretical criminal law. The other professors I was exposed to were mostly ignorant and incoherent. Worst of all were my fellow students. I had no respect for any of them – except perhaps as drinking buddies.

Even worse, many of them were likely to get better grades than I. This was a terrifying prospect. If I did not finish the first year in the top ten percent, I would not get on the law review and I would spend the rest of my law school career in a condition as close as I could imagine to living above a cleaning store.

I had started making plans to transfer. The two places I could get in were Chicago and Columbia. Susan already had definite plans to go to Columbia, which then boasted some of the great stars in English literature. I was not going to let that determine my choice.

As chance would have it, in the summer of 1961, Monrad Paulson – one of the leaders in criminal law in his generation – came from Columbia to teach a summer course at UCLA. He was a jovial, accessible fellow. I went to see him and talk about my predicament. He was very helpful without pushing too much in the Columbia direction. I told him I was planning to visit both schools before I decided. He encouraged me to contact him in New York. When I finally did, he touched me deeply by inviting me to lunch at the faculty club with his colleagues.

The factor that swayed my decision was the opportunity – which existed only at Chicago – to write one's way onto the law review, that is, to participate in an open competition, regardless of grades, in which the writers of the best essays would be selected for the prestigious journal. That appealed not only to my self-interest but also to my sense of how the world should be run. Grades should not matter as much as they did then in picking the law school elite. In the course of time, my view of these matters has prevailed in the schools around the country (affirmative action may have had something to do with it). Now, I think, all law reviews have write-on competitions.

With my career prospects the deciding factor, I left Susan at Columbia, flew into the little Midway airport on the southside of Chicago, registered at Chicago and moved into a comfortable suite by myself in the Burton Judson dormitory.

My first challenge was the writing competition. I threw

myself into it as though my life and future depended on it (and it did). I made the cut and then the real work began. I was assigned to a "rewrite man" – a third-year student whose job was to shape up the article (or get me to shape it up) for publication. His name was John Junker and my relationship with him turned out to be more intense than any I have ever had with a professor. He made me rewrite the article about ten times, which was annoying at the time, but it was the experience that taught me how to write.

There is an important point implicit here. Teachers don't have the time to invest in reading ten drafts of the same paper. A senior student with a little taste for power is more likely to do a better job. In any event, the article was finally published in 1962 and as one my profs said at the time, it was the closest experience a man could have to giving birth. That was the first of over 150 articles that have appeared in the last half-century. Beginning with the second venture, I always chose the topic myself and I always picked a philosophical theme. For example, the second, which appeared in the same Chicago Law Review three years later, was about the kind of legislation that imposes sanctions equivalent to criminal punishment and therefore requires the kind of protective trial reserved for criminal charges. This theme is still of the utmost relevance today in trying to figure out the rights of the Guantanamo detainees.

Following the first-year on the law review, Susan and I married and undertook a life-changing three-months' tour around Europe. This was the first time I was exposed to European culture on the ground and to the practical need of learning languages. Had it not been for this trip, I would not have gravitated, as I did, toward comparative law where I could continue to enjoy the same kind of experiences traveling and speaking diverse languages.

We came back to a serious student life in Chicago. Susan had finished her MA with honors at Columbia and then set about getting her teacher's certificate. The following year, 1964-65, I participated in Max Rheinstein's program in comparative law and Susan taught English at Homewood-Flossmore High School.

## *Working*

After my training in comparative law at Chicago and in Freiburg, I was ready to go on the job market. I had no idea of how to find a job. Fortunately, Max Rheinstein, the director of the comparative law program, did. A major law firm was willing to send me to Moscow as their representative, but Susan would have had to live by herself in Helsinki and we would commute back and forth. This seemed like a ridiculous plan so we passed. I was more interested in an academic position anyway. Fortunately, Rheinstein knew how the academic game worked backwards and forwards. He contacted his friend Walter Weihrauch, a German immigrant teaching at the University of Florida in Gainesville. Weihrauch contacted his friend in Freiburg, Wolfram Müller Freienfels, who promptly summoned me to his office for an interview. The interview was light. All that mattered was that I spoke German well and made some modicum of sense. This resulted in a favorable letter from Wolfram to Walter, who translated it, as he said afterwards, liberally to my advantage. Thus the old German boy network led to my getting a one year appointment, without an interview with the faculty, at the University of Florida in Gainesville. After that I was on the track and despite my innate anxieties, I had more or less made it.

My first class was in the law of copyrights. Believe it or not, I had never studied the course but was assigned to teach it. I had to bone up by reading Mel Nimmer's treatise on the subject. I was so nervous before the first class that I did not sleep a wink. I got through the class and then crashed waiting for my second class, which I believe was on civil procedure, a subject I knew equally little about. The great advantage of the case system is that you can teach just about anything by staying a few cases ahead of the students. The traditional law school teacher is not supposed to give an overview of the subject in any event.

We had an offer to stay in Florida and there were lots of advantages in the small town. The main one was Walter Weihrauch, who truly was an eccentric in the American academy.

He and his friends – notably Sanford Katz – and I had a good time together, but the small town college life did not suit my ambitions so I was receptive to my friend (and re-write man) Junker's invitation to join him at the University of Washington in Seattle. This meant a long journey by car from Florida diagonally across the country to Washington.

There they invited me to teach torts to a small group of about 30 students (most classes run closer to 100). I was discovering my love for the analysis of human wrongdoing and the challenge of probing the theory of responsibility. I flourished in the subject, which is about as close to criminal law as you can get. It was a pleasure to reunite with John Junker, this time as his equal.

Seattle is too beautiful not to swoon about. We bought a house on Capitol Hill, walking distance across various bodies of water to and from the campus. The house was located in a gorgeous and luxurious place overlooking the bays on all sides. I recall the fireplace in the bedroom, something I have never seen again. We started paying more attention to our two children, Deborah, born in Freiburg, and Rebecca in Seattle. So it seemed that we had it all – house, job, income, children. Susan had not quite solved her quest for the PhD in English but that would have solved itself had we stayed a few years.

It all fell apart in the student riots of 1968. I got involved because the faculty threatened to fire one my buddies, Phil Bilancia, for not having made adequate progress on his Chinese-English dictionary, undoubtedly a mammoth undertaking. I could not really make a difference in the dispute, even though I knew that by getting involved I was taking risks for my family. It turned out that there were some financial irregularities in Bilancia's appointment. I paid a call on the president of the university and asked him to inquire. The upshot was that the dean was fired.

As a result of the turmoil, I did not have many friends among the older faculty. The prospect of getting tenure seemed dicey. I was very happy then to get an offer from Father Robert Drinan at Boston College to cross the country for a year. As it turns out there were many of my ex-buddies from the Florida faculty who had moved to BC and they pushed through my appointment. I was thrilled to get some exposure to academic life among the elite schools in the East and therefore despite the enormous logistic problems (selling the house, etc.) I was eager to go.

We settled in Cambridge and I started hanging out at the Harvard library two or three days a week. They had a superb collection of foreign law. This was the first place I found where I could really do foreign research. Others of similar taste were attracted to the stacks so I quickly met a lot of like-minded souls. I looked up Alan Dershowitz and we became instant friends. I attended the seminar by Charles Fried on legal philosophy. I became an integral part of the school, even though two or three days a week I had to ride my bike across town to give classes at Boston College Law School. I did not mind the latter but it would not have been enough to sustain me. I was quickly developing a taste for the best and brightest.

During the year I was invited to a conference at Lake Arrowhead in California on tort theory. This is was an excellent chance to write up some views based on my having taught the class several times in Washington and again at BC. The attendees in Arrowhead were the greatest names of the time in tort and legal theory – among them Harry Kalven, Jr., Herbert Morris, Richard Wasserstrom, and Gerald Posner. I could not believe that I was included in that group and that I was expected to give a paper. As it turned out, after an initial bout of nervousness and some vomiting in the car driving up, I took it easy and felt very comfortable among the luminaries of the field.

My draft of an article turned into the first major article I published on tort law in the 1972 Harvard Law Review: "Fairness and Utility in Tort Theory." It was the first systematic attack on the economists' attempt to take over tort law as a sub-species of economic theory. But it stands virtually alone (an article by Richard Epstein about the same time also received a lot of attention). My 1972 article is the standard reference for economists who want to show that they have covered all their bases – the theory of justice as well as of efficiency for resolving tort disputes. To this day this article remains my most frequently cited work. Even though I have written more important articles in criminal law, they have not outcited this one and I have never scored with another major piece in tort theory.

It took me about four years of moving around the country before I could get assigned to teach a course in criminal law. Two years in Seattle, one year at Boston College, and finally the invitation to UCLA in the fall of 1969. I loved the idea of teaching criminal law. I went into class with a fury – banging my wedding ring on the desk, marching up and down aisles, trying to out-Germanify von Caemmerer. The students were taken aback and fell in love with the subject. In those two years of teaching criminal law, three of my students were transported by the excitement of the subject – Sharon Byrd, who teaches today in Erlangen, Germany; David J. Cohen, a professor in the Rhetoric Department in Berkeley; and Paul Robinson, one of the senior people in the field of criminal law today. We hung around together after class, frequented bars together, they came over for dinner and met my family. It was the brewing of a cult.

Not only did they commit themselves to the field but they all had topics to which they have remained faithful. Sharon Byrd took on the field of battered women and self-defense. David Cohen more or less invented the modern field of ancient Greek law, which he analyzed on the basis of current jurisprudential constructs. Paul Robinson balked at my argument in class that self-defense must be supported by an intention to act in self-defense. He has made a career out of defending the principle of objective self-defense – or self-defense unsupported by knowledge of the intended attack. Of course all three of these scholars have written other books as well.

In those early years of teaching I must have carried an infectious academic bug, but in 1972, five years after the Six Day War finally took its toll on our conscience, we left to spend a year teaching at the Hebrew University in Jerusalem. I had offers to return to Harvard and Yale but we had no idea what to do.

In Jerusalem for the year, I happened upon two important students: Mordechai Kremnitzer in my seminar on comparative criminal law and Miri Gur Aryeh in my class on the law of theft. Both of them became professors of criminal law. Think about the odds of all this happening. In four years in Los Angeles and Jerusalem, from 1969 to 1973, I generated a passion for academic work in five students, all of whom succeeded in becoming leading professors in their fields. I have not had a similar success in any analogous segment of five or even ten or fifteen years of my career as a teacher.

After the year in Israel, returning to the US was very difficult. Our children had learned the language. My wife wanted to stay in Israel as a committed Zionist, regardless of her professional advantages in the US. Irrationally, I found the pull of Harvard irresistible. All those years of being conditioned on the career conveyor belt were hard to keep in perspective. Harvard called, I had to go. It was probably the worst decision of my life.

There were a few impressive people at Harvard, in particular, Roberto Unger, Morton Horowitz, and Duncan Kennedy. They were a clique who called themselves, half seriously, the party of humanity. The words and ideas of Unger's lectures were overpowering. We applauded at the end of every lecture. He kindly invited me to refute his views but I had nothing to say. My only refutation was in form. I tried to mock his style by doing the opposite. If he paced the room, I sat still. If he spoke bombastically, I replied in subdued tones. The year turned out to be a disappointment because at the end I did not receive an offer to stay. We limped home to LA to pick up the threads at UCLA.

We drove across the country, which had its pleasures. We could stop and visit a friend practically every day of the journey – something not possible today with the thinning out of college friendships. The consolation of our return was a new beautiful home in Santa Monica, the down payment subsidized in part by our four elders, my mother, her husband Meyer Naxon, Alyse and Karl Laemmle. It was a great gift, a promise of a new life in California.

Both Susan and I had unfinished business and needed the time to get down to work. She had yet to finish her PhD in English. She signed up immediately to study with some good people specializing in Edmund Spencer's *The Fairie Queen*. She loved the material, middle English and all. I had my project cut out for me. On our last day in Cambridge, Roberto Unger's parting words were: "You have to write a book!"

His reasons were not clear but I took his point to be that I had acquired a sophisticated body of comparative legal material but nobody in the US understood it. I had to make my expertise accessible to others.

## *The Books*

From the return to Santa Monica in the fall of 1974, I could think only about writing The Book – the one that would be large enough and comprehensive enough to establish a new field of comparative criminal law. It took me two years to set up the conditions for writing. In this time the leading law publisher of the time, Little, Brown offered me a contract. I received a grant for time off from the American Council of Learned Societies. I built a desk out of two doors to fit comfortably in my study, the back corner room of the house. The circumstances for writing could not have been better.

Before the onset of my labor, in the summer of 1976, we – Susan, Rebecca, and I – visited H.L.A. Hart at his home in Cornwall. He had been Morris's tutor and came to UCLA one day to visit Morris. We met and he took a liking to me. The week with him was deeply illuminating. We sat on his porch every morning drinking tea with toast and discussing every idea that had occurred to me in nearly 15 years of thinking about law. He was convinced that I had to write the book intensely and quickly, as he had written *The Concept of Law* in 1961. I kept his advice in mind. I woke up refreshed after the trip to LA and sat down and started the first chapter on theft.

No one had ever written a book on criminal law by starting with theft. First, the subject is a specific crime and usually, on the Continent, writers begin with the general part, namely the general theory of offense and defenses. I was signaling off the bat that the book would be contrarian. And it was. No one had, either in the US or in Europe, written a book about criminal law in which they treated German, French, Soviet, and the common law on a par, as equally important sources of the general principles of criminal law. Criminal law has always been parochial and nationalistic – not intentionally but by default of the educational system. Their own law is all that lawyers learn in order to practice in the local courts.

I typed the first draft on an Olympic portable typewriter I borrowed from Susan, usually about 2000 words a day, then I would take a bike ride down to the beach to relax. I came back and read the draft onto a tape which I then took to a professional typist in the neighborhood. The system worked beautifully, in almost complete autonomy from UCLA. I did not even see Herb Morris for a couple of months. He was thrilled when I told him, mid-semester, about the progress I was making.

I was unsure of the title. I had originally thought of something like *Criminal Law: Policies and Principles*. Susan bequeathed me the name *Rethinking Criminal Law*, a very felicitous choice. Since then the use of the word "Rethinking" in the title has become something of a cliché. There are dozens of titles in law that use the word. But I was first, at least in law. Clifford Geertz had already used the word in a variety of titles in anthropology.

My immediate reaction to publishing *Rethinking Criminal Law* in 1978 was exhaustion. I decided to get my mind off law by learning Japanese, which occupied me for the next several years.

The impact of *Rethinking* on the external world was much different from what I expected. All of a sudden foreign scholars began to take me very seriously. Germans invited me to their conferences. Japanese scholars came to visit me simply because they heard that an American had mastered the European way of thinking about criminal law. Because I was learning their language I was delighted to visit them and give lectures around Japan (mostly in English, with the first line always in Japanese). On a social level I functioned well in Japanese but the more I learned about their legal culture, the less interested I was. It all seemed derivative of the German system of thought, with word for word translations of the key concepts.

The impact in the US was much less significant. I have a lot of respect for the practical knowledge of my colleagues about how the process works, that is, the impact of plea bargaining, evidentiary rules, sentencing and other operative matters that Continental scholars ignore. The difference can be summed up by the relationship of criminal law to criminal procedure. On the Continent these are two entirely different fields, only the former is taken seriously as a subject of scholarly study. In the US, procedure and substance are inseparable. The importance of procedure is magnified by the attention the Supreme Court has given to the interpretation of the Fourth, Fifth, and Sixth Amendments. No constitution in the world takes these issues – right to counsel, jury trial, privilege against self-incrimination, right to confront witnesses – as seriously as in the US. European and Asian scholars of substantive law almost never pay heed to the related procedural issues. In *Rethinking Criminal Law* I offer some bridges between the subjects but there was much left to say.

Writing *Rethinking* had such a powerful impact on me that it was almost ten years before I published another book. When it became clear in the summer of 1986 that Bernhard Goetz was going to trial for having shot and wounded four young Blacks on the subway in December 1984, I sensed an immediate calling. The facts were exquisitely designed to probe the issue of self-defense. One of the four young Blacks asked Goetz for five dollars. Goetz asked for confirmation of the request and then immediately pulled out a concealed Smith & Wesson .38 revolver and shot five times, hitting all four, and permanently injuring the last of the four, Darrell Cabey. The day it happened the case was headline news in New York and the rest of the country soon picked up on the subway drama.

By a twist of fate, the presiding Judge Stephen Crane was a friend of mine from college, even from the same fraternity. We were close enough to make phone contact. I called him immediately. He invited me to come down as an observer of the trial. I was there every day and privy to the most secret meetings. Anytime the judge was there, I was there. We often had lunch together alone. Counsel trusted me as though I were the judge's clerk. They knew of the friendship and obviously did not want to irritate the judge by challenging his judgment. They had no idea what I would write, so perhaps the lawyers thought they had as much to win as to lose by my presence. They must have also enjoyed the sense that their role in history was being recorded for future generations.

The whole experience was a great treat. I had time off from classes for another project. I rode my bicycle downtown every day and parked it at 1 Church Street, the courthouse. I became friendly with all the reporters and the courtroom artists (no TV in the courtroom in those days).

My approach in the Goetz book was to remain a "fly on the wall" – as impartial as possible. There was one incident when I felt that the judge was tolerating injustice in the courtroom and I felt compelled to intervene. The story is worth telling.

As in many cases of excessive self-defense to fend off a robbery by strangers, there is a racial component weighing on the facts. The aggressors are usually of a minority race and the defender of the dominant race seeking to protect their property. There are famous cases of this sort in Israel, Spain, and elsewhere. The minority-outsider race of the aggressors increases the component of fear. When race is considered, the shooting appears more reasonable than it would otherwise.

The problem is encapsulated in formulating the reasonable person test under the circumstances. The use of defensive force is legal if a reasonable person would have done the same. The problem is whether the reasonable person should reflect the racial factors of the case. If yes, it is easier to secure an acquittal for the defendant. Usually criminal lawyers are in favor; the constitutional lawyers are opposed.

At one point in the Goetz trial, the judge decided at the behest of the defense to stage a recreation of the shooting. The main point to prove by this staging was how the bullet traveled from Goetz's gun to the victims. When the parts for the victims were ready to be played, the defendants called on four Guardian Angels, who were young tough Black kids standing in their insignia T-shirts at the back of the room. (In the 1980s, the Guardian Angels were a group of Black teens who rode the subway in order to maintain peace and order.) The young men started to take their places and it was apparent that the defense wanted to recreate for the jury how fearful it felt for Goetz to be surrounded by four young Black men. Fortunately, it was time to break for the day. I immediately spoke to the judge and he agreed that the racial element had to eliminated. When court reconvened, the part of the four victims were played by white middle-aged courtroom guards. The defense heard of my interactions with the judge on this issue and never trusted me again.

The Goetz book has turned out to be a good teaching vehicle on the law of self-defense and on the nuts and bolts of running a trial. For that reason it has sold well and been translated into numerous languages. As I related in the Spanish chapter, Bracha's first contact with me was reading my translated words in the Spanish edition.

Looking back on the series of books I wrote in the quarter of a century after I finished *Rethinking*, I think each book was a reaction to some external stimulus in my life. The Goetz book, we know, was occasioned by the trial that began in the spring of

1987 in downtown Manhattan.

When I published *Rethinking* I knew there must have been important aspects of the criminal law I was leaving out. I was reminded of just how myopic my view was when the riots of the *madres* and *abuelas* (mothers and grandmothers) in Buenos Aires in the late 1970s came to my attention. I had not thought about the victims' side of the equation. But it is not an easy matter to formulate a theory of the criminal that gives proper due to the defendant's culpability and the victim's yearning to see the wrongdoer punished. At the time, four groups were clamoring for justice in the US – gays, Blacks, orthodox Jews, and women victims of sexual assault. The gays were outraged that Dan White, who killed Mayor George Moscone as well as the first open gay politician Harvey Milk, was sentenced to the lesser charge of manslaughter instead of murder.

The orthodox Jews of Brooklyn took to the streets after someone who murdered one of their own received a juvenile penalty. The Rodney King case was the most famous of them all. Four LA white policemen beat up Rodney King, a Black man suspected of speeding, and they were tried in a suburban court with an all-white jury. Not surprisingly, the officers were acquitted. Riots broke out all over Los Angeles. In addition there were numerous female rape victims who never saw justice in their cases.

I noted for the first time the way in which the English language assists us in expressing the difference between offenders and victims. In most languages there is no clear distinction between justice and fairness, but in English the distinction tracks the cleavage between aggressor and victim. The defendants want only a fair trial; they have no interest in justice, which might lead to a severe penalty for their crimes. Only victims clamor for justice. In their famous slogan, "No Justice, no peace."

There is a germ of loyalty in these strong attachments of gays to gay victims, Jews to Jewish victims, Blacks to Black victims, and women to female victims of rape. The implicit challenge is to explore the theme of loyalty on its own – detached from criminal justice. Two experiences led me in that direction. The first experience was being trapped at the Canadian/American border without a passport sometime in the early 1980s.

In the 1940s it was common for illegal immigrants to the US to go to Canada and then return, thus establishing a legal date of entry. In fact, my father did this in 1941 when after many years as an illegal resident, he decided that my birth required regularization of his papers. This must have become relevant in his thinking when the US entered the war in Europe. He had an easy time crossing the border without a passport in 1941 but forty years later it was another story.

The problem was that when I approached the border – artificially drawn in the Toronto airport – the guard asked where I was born. I flashed back to my father's accent in Hungarian and answered "Chicaaaago," as he would have said it. Well, it looked like curtains for me. My New York driver's license could not redeem me – only the passport itself, which I had left at home, would suffice. No papers, no entry. No counsel could have helped me. Finally, in the spirit of play, as I was becoming desperate, the guard asked me to recite the Pledge of Allegiance from memory. I actually did it. "I pledge allegiance to the flag of the United States of America and to the Republic for which it stands, one nation, under God, with liberty and justice for all." In virtually all schools in the US, young children recite this pledge. That you can do it is a pretty good sign that you are an American. This prompted me to think about other cultural bonds that establish the identity of native residents. In fact oaths and pledges of this sort are not so common. And it is a little tricky trying to identity someone as, say, Argentine.

The other, more philosophical stimulus for a study of loyalty was a question from David Hartman when I first called upon him in Jerusalem and told him that I had been working on Kant: "Fletcher, don't you know that Kant's universalistic ethics cannot accommodate special relationships?" Hartman had in mind the covenant between God and the Jewish people, but the same point applies to friendship, love, and loyalty to country. Prompted by these two stimuli, it did not take me too long to finish writing about these virtues in my book, *Loyalty: An Essay on the Morality of Relationships* (1993), which appeared as well in several languages abroad.

Since 1993, this special relationship of loyalty – of preferential treatment – has acquired a lot of philosophical attention. And some animosity. I recall that my German colleagues were a bit shocked that I would address a topic so close to the sentiments of Fascism. The German translation of my book on loyalty features a cover showing a young very mid-Western couple reverently addressing the American flag. That was undoubtedly something very incorrect, politically, about my implicitly veering off in the direction of nationalism and patriotism. Yet in some quarters the book carried an important message. Many rabbis and Jewish communal workers have sought to use the book as a way of developing great solidarity in their organizations. I am not sure why, but William Safire at the Times loved the book and cited it often.

The intervention of an attractive fellowship in 1995 gave me some to time to think and ponder my future lines of work. The German *Wissenschaftspreis* supported me for several years, a few months at a time, in the Panorama Hotel over the rooftops of Freiburg. I developed the habit of sitting by the pool, having a festive breakfast served to me every morning on linen and relaxing and writing by the pool for several hours. After writing I would swim or hike or cycle in the Black Forest adjacent to the hotel. When I needed to see people, I rode down to the Max Planck Institute in the center of town. This was undoubtedly one of the more pleasurable experiences of my life. In those sojourns in the Panorama, two books in a series I had planned on the basic concepts of various branches of law. I settled for the *Basic Concepts of Legal Thought* and the *Basic Concepts of Criminal Law*. The latter has become one of my most successful books, translated into several languages and used widely by students in the United States.

Shortly thereafter I expanded my work on loyalty and merged my thinking with national politics. The result was a theory of the legal transformations wrought by the Civil War. This book, *Our Secret Constitution: How Lincoln Redefined American Democracy,* received a surprising amount of critical attention. The American Association of Publishers picked it as the best book on law published in 2001.

The first year of the new Millennium was quiet – at least until September 11. It was clear to me at the time that the attacks of that magnitude would shape my work for many years. My first problem, which I wrote about right away in an op-ed piece, was whether to think of the attacks as an act of war or an act of crime. There was a tendency to want it both ways. The military responded in Afghanistan as though 9/11 were a declaration of war by the Taliban. But the federal government had no desire to follow the law of war in deciding the treatment to accord those subsequently captured on the battlefield. The detainees, of course, wanted to be treated as prisoners of war, as would be required by the war conventions, but instead the government prevailed with new nomenclature – enemy combatants – a term made up by the Department of Defense to cover the new kind of irregular fighters in the field.

The problem dates back to the Hague Convention of 1999, which prescribes four conditions for a fighter to be treated as a combatant. Those fighting out of uniform or not carrying their arms opening fail to qualify. The problem, then, is what are they? The issues of proper classification and its legal consequences has haunted us to this day. We still cannot decide when the writ of habeas corpus, the jury trial, the conventions of war, or Uniform Code of Military Justice should apply.

As late as 2006, we had a major crisis in the Supreme Court about whether Salim Ahmad Hamdan, bin Ladin's personal driver for the year surrounding the attack, should be tried under the law of war or the criminal law. The government obviously preferred to invoke the law of war. It provided them with easier procedural options – namely a trial in a military commission instead of a federal court.

The charge against Hamdan was conspiracy to engage in terrorist acts as a violation of the law of war. I was called into the case on the issue of conspiracy. Comparative and international insights carried the day. On the basis of my brief, four Justices, led by Justice Stevens, held that the law of war did not include the crime of conspiracy. We got a fifth vote from Justice Kennedy on a procedural question. For me personally, the case was a surprising victory for the power of theoretical analysis in the law. What mattered in the final analysis was not policy, not politics, not preferences, but the history and structure of the law itself. It might have been possible to argue successfully for the opposite conclusion but in fact the government was caught off guard, as often is true in highly theoretical cases.

*Hamdan* typified my interests in the decade after 9/11. The most significant book to appear then was *Romantics at War: Glory and Guilt in the Age of Terrorism.* The problem was to address the role of Romantics in our thinking about war. There is no doubt that the Romantic impulse – the search for meaning and a noble life amidst the shooting and killing – was a powerful factor before World War I and behind the wars since 9/11. The only problem is that the Romantic impulse wears off quickly. The brothers may be exultant when they go off in arms together but as soon as they see their buddies' heads blown off, their Romantic sentiments sour quickly.

At the turn of the Millennium I had felt that I had run dry on my standard repertoire of subjects. I tried one more tome on criminal law – *The Grammar of Criminal Law: American, Comparative, and International*. It is a hodge-podge about language and basic concepts of a universal system of criminal law. The reception to the book was polite but not enthusiastic. It convinced me that new ideas about criminal law would have to come from a new generation.

The best thing for criminal lawyers to do in the next few generations is to concentrate on the development of international criminal law and bring to bear the theoretical lessons of the past on the issues now pending in the Hague. This is important and there are already many signs that the young staffers coming out of the ad hoc tribunals and the ICC will concentrate on this rudimentary work to be done.

For myself, my future lies partly elsewhere. A curious combination of factors led to me believe in early 2000 that I could write fiction, and in particular, fiction about the scenes we encounter all the time in courtrooms, in jail, and in the daily interactions of lawyers, judges, clients, and victims. There is great drama lurking in these encounters and the task of the writer is to elicit it.

My first novel, *The Bond,* was a gratifying success – for me at least. The publisher would have liked to sell a few more copies, and perhaps will, if we can convince instructors to incorporate the novel in the way they teach comparative and legal thought. Those who read *The Bond* come away with a sense of having experienced a gripping tale as well as an immersion in legal education.

I have planned as my next book a study in the law of war called the *Law of War and its Pathologies*. After this act of service to my profession I will try my hand again at fiction – this time about the Bible and a Bible lesson that takes place in Jerusalem and inadvertently serves to solve a murder.

## *The People*

In the course of this story about my seven languages I have concentrated on narrative and have not spent enough time on the people who influenced the shape of my life. There are many people who spoke to me in other than the seven languages and many colleagues, family, and friends for whom language was not the issue. This is a quick series of portraits of the personalities that made a difference to me – particularly in my earlier years.

I must begin my mentioning my family – leaving their Hungarian sides to that chapter. My father, Miklós, communicated support and love no matter what I chose to do. He was a simple man with Communist beliefs caught in a capitalist grind, but it could have been much worse. He ran a few lower-priced, informal hotels, which enabled him to schmooze with the guests as he brought in his daily bread. He would not have survived in a Sheraton chain.

In 1960, the Regina Hotel had the honor of hosting the Oregon delegation to the Democratic convention being held downtown, just a few miles from the Regina. There were few hotel rooms available in those days, so there wasn't much choice. I worked the night shift then. It was a great treat to hear all the stories of the semi-drunk Oregonians as they came late at night. Their minds weren't much on JFK or competition but on the wild time they were having away from home.

The hotel defined my father's life. He always called to find out how many empty rooms there were each night. He established a close friendship with the Philippine houseboy who worked in the hotel. Somehow the hotel gave him a chance to think he was a man of the people while still playing the role of the capitalist.

My mother, Fanny, could not have cared less about politics. Her arena was her friends, the higher the status the better. She was most deeply engaged when she was preparing to receive company. The kitchen was filled with baked goods, the best in the world so far as I knew. When the company was finally assembled around the table, my mother was a master at soliciting conversation. She would turn to various of the Hungarian gentlemen and say, "Now, Ernő, will you tell us a funny story," or "Pista, tell us something about your recent trip to Europe."

I enjoyed these semi-rehearsed presentations. I haven't seen anything like it since.

In my first marriage, for most of the 22 years, our Shabbat table consisted of Susan, Deborah, Rebecca, myself, perhaps our in-laws Alyce and Kurt, perhaps my mother and Meyer, and perhaps some friends. Susan always made a magnificent meal. She brought to bear to our marriage her extraordinary knowledge of English literature. My eyes were opened to many works I didn't even know existed. The marriage was something like a seminar about law, philosophy, English, and related matters. Yet we failed at the essential test of coming to grips with our feelings and communicating, as a man and wife must, in order to survive.

Deborah was always a super bright child but easily bored by family events. I always enjoyed playing with her from her first to her ninth year. Yet there was something missing in the dynamic of the family – perhaps something as simply defined as love. She needed more of it and we did not know how to give it. Deborah developed an obsession with Kenya because we once had a Kenyan gardener who gave her a poster of the country. She learned the language Swahili and went there to study for her junior year of college – in the long run not a good plan because she had enormous difficulties readapting to the US afterwards.

After her second stint in Kenya – this time teaching with her daughter Rachel in tow – she came back and decided to get married. She is a resourceful woman and within a short time found a very suitable mate, Warren Blum. Together they have a four-year-old daughter, Esther.

Rebecca received attention from everyone. She was a naturally popular child. She learned Hebrew well and spent several years in Israel. While she was there she started singing lessons and her teacher convinced her that she had a superb voice. As a result she went to cantorial school and acquired a craft for earning a living. The sad part of her story is that she remained committed to becoming a great singer. I imagine that this is a constant source of frustration while she is an excellent cantor and could do much more in Judaism if she so decided. She has a natural gift with people and a very quick literary mind. She must be aware of all this as she continues on her path in life.

I did not know my ex-wife Susan's parents, Alyse and Kurt, very long, but they were impressive people in their own right.

Alyse had a charisma rarely matched in women her age. She used it effectively to raise money for Israel and also in making a great success out of selling insurance with her husband. Kurt was more of a quiet intellectual and actually influential in instilling in me a sense that I could be an intellectual. He read one of my papers – I believe it was about the problem of analogy in law – and he commented immediately that he saw the scholar in me. He had no idea this little piece of support was important to me.

Kurt and his brother Max were in the business of importing foreign films to the US. During the Nazi years they had spent time in Germany and France and therefore knew the languages and learned the distribution business. Their first big success was *Un Homme et une Femme*, a French love story that had an overwhelming success in V.O. (the original language). With some exceptions, most imported films since then have been shown in the original language with subtitles. Most Europeans, by the way, still dub, even on television, which makes it harder for children to learn foreign languages.

Bobbie (presumably Barbara), Max's wife, was my primary Russian contact in the family. I met with her from time to time for tea, Russian, and gossip. My impression was that she built the foreign film industry in LA by inviting over the leading critics for the LA Times for a little "koffee and kuchen," Viennese style. They got the idea: European culture could sell in the US.

At the other end of the spectrum, you might say, were the hippies Sandra, Susan's sister, and her husband Yoram Getzler. Sandra was an artist and like the long line of artists in our family, believed that the world owed her a living – well if not the world, then at least her parents. Yoram and Sandra lived for a while in the mountains of Big Sur with other hippies and then sought land far away from it all in the middle of Colorado. Despite their isolation and the relative deprivation of city comforts, their three kids grew up to be very accomplished. Lila is a lawyer, a graduate of Stanford, but seems to be proud of getting canned from one of her first jobs for refusing to wear shoes. Avila has a PhD in

English from Berkeley and teaches in the Midwest. Yutan (a made up name to sound both Indian and Israeli) has degrees in science and carries on his research in a lab in Ohio.

In the other corner of the family, the intriguing characters are the two that debated the Hungarian and Jewish nature of the family, Frank and Paul. Frank, 15 years my senior, has darted in and out of my story from the days our fathers were friends in Chicago. Paul and I are the same age, we grew up together, always a little competitive. He was always smarter but that gave me an edge to try harder. For the last 20 years or so he has had a good gig updating the pocket parts (the annual supplements) of the book of essays on international copyright he put together at the behest of my friend Mel Nimmer. He takes a few cases on the side and makes a living – nothing too stressful. But the field is small and he is probably one of the world's leading experts. He lives on the top of a canyon on the West Side of LA with a pool in his backyard and mountain walks at the doorstep. He stays in excellent physical shape and with his wife Susan he makes sure he enjoys the finer things of life.

Almost a daughter to me, my niece Cheryl and I bonded in her childhood, when her mother was ill and her family life in difficulty. We have stayed close and now I cherish my relationships with her husband Richard and her daughter Lily, named in honor of my sister Lillian.

My personal debts to my colleagues are too long to be sure of not omitting someone significant. The most important influence on my thinking and my work was, of course, Herbert Morris at UCLA, a legal philosopher and theoretical criminal lawyer. Beyond these labels his true love was literature, his favorite seminar being on law and literature. He taught me everything but failed to implant his devotion to literature. This was my fault, I suppose. I always felt saddled by a mathematical mind and therefore essentially incompetent in thinking about literature. (When I was writing *The Bond*, I told myself that writing, which I felt confident about, and literary criticism, were entirely separate domains.) My perpetual lag in literature was compensated for, in part, by Rella's reading her poems to me. They are now conveniently collected in a little volume called *Time Pieces* (originally published 1966), still available on Amazon.

My favorite poem in the collection retells the ceremony of her son David's receiving his driver's license from the California DMV. It begins:

We have come to the edge of the Sacred,
We have come for the High Ritual,
We have come for the Test,
In the kiva of the DMV.

The poem ends with celebrating David's passing the test and thus entering into manhood – California style:

LOOK AT HIM. THIS ONE,
MY SON. HE HAS PASSED....
For he has met and conquered
Judgments of the faceless ones.

Rella was the greatest artist of the family but there were many who had a good eye for beauty. The strain of art collecting in the family, alas, did not rub off on me. The leaders of the group were Richard (Dickie) Berk, Karen, my aunt Margaret, Lola (Alex's wife) and to some extent my mother. My mother had an excellent collection of 19th century Hungarian pastoral art, which she bequeathed to me. The others went into more exotic and valuable areas of art. Margaret and Béla had acquired a first-rate collection of contemporary masters as well as a collection of carved ivory, which they would only show to special guests.

I have strayed from my task of mentioning the personal influences I encountered in academia. Mel Nimmer was a great friend and mentor before he died prematurely. I recall one conversation in the late 1970s when I was thinking of taking a job offer in the Netherlands. Having run out of other arguments why we should stay in LA, he asked whether I was not afraid that the Russians might march. This was his style. His dry wit triumphed – even when he was suffering from a brain tumor and his head was heavily bandaged.

The other senior member of the UCLA faculty who had an impact on me was David Mellinkoff. In the 1960s, David had written a very interesting book called *The Language of the Law*, the new paperback edition published in 2004. He brought together my two great loves – language and law. Of course, I read the book before meeting David for an interview (pay heed, young scholars, this is always a good thing to do) and no doubt he was a major supporter of my appointment at UCLA. His wife Ruth wrote a series of gripping books about Jewish themes in art history – books like *The Mark of Cain*, which traced and analyzed this image in the history of Western art. She also wrote at least a half dozen cook books and gave the best dinner parties I have ever attended.

My office neighbor for many years was Gary Schwarz. A thin door separated our two offices. Gary was blessed with a booming voice. There were no secrets between us. We also shared a love for tort law and had endless conversations about the material. Jim Krier joined the conversation trying to convince us of the relevance of economic analysis. Sadly, Gary was stricken with cancer and joined other loves of my life – Gerry, Mel, and Rella – who were taken from me much too early.

When I moved to Columbia in 1984, my close colleagues were my contemporaries – Bruce Ackerman, Meir Dan-Cohen, Andrzej Rapaczynski. Only the latter stayed in New York. Among the senior faculty, John Hazard was notably kind to me. We co-taught the course on Soviet law several times and he generally watched out for me. I owe a great deal to the generation before me – Herb, Mel, David at UCLA, Hazard at Columbia – for making me feel I had a role to play in academia. Bruce and I stayed close even though he was a bumpy two-hour train ride away. His series of volumes on American constitutional history defined my view of the significant stages of constitutional evolution in the US. Although all my colleagues in those early years were committed academics, Bruce brought more enthusiasm and intellectual commitment than most.

Eventually, however, one grows out of the dependent state when senior scholars show concern and offer guidance for your future. The cycle turns. Fortunately, it turned in time for me, in the year 2001, to discover a whole new life based not only 9/11 but also on a new slate of courses in which I would be called upon to play a leadership role. The International Criminal Court's coming into force in July 1, 2002, meant that the work I had done on international and comparative criminal law would take on new importance. This has proven to be true with the Court relying almost exclusively on *Rethinking Criminal Law* as its authority on the basic principles of law applicable in diverse countries.

Anticipating greater reliance on self-defense in the wars of the future, a former student, now Professor Jens Ohlin and I published a book in 2008 entitled *Defending Humanity: When Force is Justified and Why.*

The sudden explosion of LLM students in US law courses meant that we would need new courses to satisfy their needs. I was in the perfect position to respond to these new demands in legal education.

I conceived of a new course for the massive group of entering LLM students that would give them a comparative overview of the first year curriculum in three weeks. The survey course – Comparative Introduction to American Law – offers me my most enjoyable teaching experience of the year. The course led to a 2005 casebook with another former student, now Professor Steve Sheppard, that carries the title, *American Law in a Global Context: The Basics.*

In most classes I struggle to be innovative and different. In this class the point is to bring legal studies down to the level of the students, struggling as I once did, with the particularities of the common law. Because I know their legal background in the "civil law," I can speak to them in their conceptual language. I begin each hour with respect for the superior wisdom and experience of the students and they often finish the course by returning the same compliment to me.

My understanding of civil law thinking has benefited greatly from my conversations with Bracha, who, as a skilled practitioner of Argentine law, has often challenged me on both theoretical and practical levels.

When I write their multiple-choice exam, I become one of the faceless ones. As in David's experience at the DMV, I am one of the unnamed examiners who must decide whether they PASS – whether they will be accepted into the inner circle of legal warriors.

The fears of many of the students are captured in Rella's evocation of the Indian judges, those who must pick the novitiates who will be accepted as full members of the tribe. As the lines continue from the poem:

> They rise from the earth's throat
> To prance down rocky beasts of fields.
> We see them from miles away,
> White specks on the mountain,
> Dancing, leaping, strafing the brush,
> With white leather whips as they come
> The silent, waiting pueblo:
> Eerie judges,
> Punishers sent by the gods.

It takes a poet's eye to see an examination in this way. But let us benefit from Rella's conferring this drama on our humble tasks. I accept the role of being one of the faceless ones. The attention shifts to the triumph of the braves, for they pass. They are the ones of whom we can say: They did it. They mastered another legal system. They entered the select few who will lead in a multi-national world.

Made in the USA
Monee, IL
12 May 2026

49989645R00115